The *ORIGINAL* Blue Danube Cookbook

The ~ORIGINAL Blue

Fine Recipes

An original collection

compiled and translated from

Lancaster-Miller Publishers, Berkeley, California

Danube Cookbook
of the Old Austrian Empire
From Boiled Potatoes to Sacher Torte

of Austrian, Hungarian, and Bohemian recipes
handwritten notes of his mother by *MAX KNIGHT*

Illustrated by WOLFGANG LEDERER

© 1979 by Max Knight

Library of Congress
Catalog Card Number: 79-65488
ISBN: 0-89581-008-5

First Printing: 1967
Second Printing: 1968
Third Printing: 1979

Typography by
THE SHIELDS' PRESS, SAN FRANCISCO, CALIFORNIA

Printed in the United States of America

Contents

A Birthday Present

WHEN THE AUSTRIAN EMPIRE COLLAPSED in 1918, three price-less cultural treasures survived the catastrophe: the venerable name of Austria itself — applied to a smaller area after the independence of Hungary, Czechoslovakia, and other parts of the realm; the imperial palaces, galleries, museums, collections and gardens — they were nationalized; and my mother's handwritten cookbook. Had it been published earlier, World War I would undoubtedly never have been fought, because the powerful statesmen would have been distracted from politics, satisfied with a world made palatable to them by their wives using the Blue Danube recipes.

There are Austrian, Hungarian, Bohemian, Serbian, and Polish cookbooks, so why one more?

First, because this cookbook presents "imperial" dishes — the finest of those developed not only in Austria proper, but those developed also by the individual nationalities that made up the former Austrian Empire and commonly served in Vienna: Hungarian goulash, Bohemian dumplings, Polish hot fish sauce, and many others. The title of this book was chosen to indicate the multinationality of these Empire dishes: Johann Strauss's beloved Danube connected the two capitals of the former Dual Monarchy, Vienna and Budapest.

Second, because every lowly beef soup, every dish here described, has gone through my mother's testing process. Her dinner parties used to be the talk among our friends; many of her recipes, especially the desserts, are never-published family treats created by her or handed down by tradition; the principal virtue of her cooking was not this or that sensational dish, but her own little touches, the result of a sensitive taste.

Her emphasis was on quality not cosmetics. When she made a birthday cake for me, what was under the frosting was important, not gaudily colored sugar roses on top of it. Expert though she was, she regarded herself as a student all her life, reading, clipping, and collecting the recipes printed in newspapers. Every morning in my native Vienna, even before my mother arose, my Aunt Alice would show up, sit by her bed, and hold a war council on the meals to be cooked that day. Aunt Alice was mother's peer in the art of the taste buds, and the two women were forever experimenting with new nuances. As a youngster I often mocked my Aunt Alice for her ungrammatical stock phrase: "Und dann gibbich hinein . . . ," inadequately translated as: "And then I put in . . ." There would be a pinch of this and that and, particularly, a specific method to improve a dish.

The happy results of these discussions and try-outs all went into a much-thumbed handwritten cookbook whose marbleized cover is, in my memory, a symbol of my childhood. Long after I was a grown man, my mother still wrote in that same book, several pages in it covered with my crayon drawings — the beautiful white sheets having been too tempting for the young artist to resist.

My mother prepared her formal dinner parties carefully. The day after those dinners, the telephone rang constantly. The ladies wanted the recipes. My mother, generous with her discoveries and methods, discussed the procedures at length on the wall telephone. When the ladies tried out the recipes and were not satisfied with the results, there were more telephone follow-ups. What had gone wrong? Like a doctor my mother would diagnose the situation. Had the lady done this and that correctly? The cooking time and the amount of ingredients were checked. Sometimes, to bring out the finer points, my mother would demonstrate her cooking. She was patient in answering questions, but never stopped marveling why people were disappointed when they had not followed her recipe. I remember a young lady complaining that her vanilla "Kipferl," prepared from mother's recipe — or so she claimed — did not turn out. "Yours were so much better, Mrs. Kühnel," the lady said, "why?" When mother was through checking, it turned out the lady had used margarine instead of butter, vanilla extract instead of vanilla beans, and peanuts instead of almonds.

The cookbook with the marbleized cover survived the second World War as well as the first. It traveled to the

United States, but it still was not finished. Aunt Alice was long gone, but new refinements were added to the book nevertheless and even a few new American recipes were included: The Blue Danube had reached the Pacific Ocean when Mother Kühnel settled in her little house in Albany, California.

The time for elegant dinner parties had passed now, and her art could be appreciated only when she invited a small circle of friends to a Vienna Jause or her grandchildren, my wife, and me to a birthday party. But, much as we appreciated her treats on those special occasions, the value of her art was to make the every-day meals tastier and more enjoyable, to give them the full dimension of one of life's pleasures. Enjoying a carefully prepared meal was entirely comparable to listening to good music or reading a good book.

As my mother's eightieth birthday approached, I decided, as a tribute to her, to preserve the results of decades of "Und dann gibbich hinein." The book was transcribed, typed, translated from its original German into English, edited, and, finally, privately printed. I needed all my training as an editor of the University of California Press to get the manuscript through its many stages, to interview my mother many times to supplement the instructions, and to clarify points that seemed "perfectly clear" to her as she had put them down in that book.

So the result is not a professional-scientific book on the culinary arts — it's a "mother's cookbook" rooted in the kitchen. The measurements, for example, are not always internally consistent — in one recipe 4 ounces are equated with 140 grams, in another with 150 grams; in the conversion process, mother, for convenience, sometimes rounded up the figures up or down.

When I asked my mother for some advice on cooking that could apply to the preparation of all dishes, she said: "Cook with love; your family will taste it."

Berkeley, California, 1965   MAX KNIGHT

Postscript

More than 14 years have passed since the lines above were written. My mother's delight as she opened the wrapped first copy of her own book on that evening, the happy shaking of her head in disbelief as she saw her own handwriting in print, are among the golden memories of my life. The book was a gift that lasted first for weeks, then for months, then for years, as she mailed copies to her friends and collected their appreciative letters. She had many friends, but even she could not give away more than a hundred copies. I had one thousand printed, and I expected to have nine hundred copies sitting on my shelf for the rest of her and my life. But word got around, the newspapers picked up the story of the son who gave his mother her own cookbook on her eightieth birthday, and resquests for it came in — incredibly for a privately printed little book — from every state of the union. The nine hundred were soon gone, I had another thousand printed, and those were soon gone too. But for all the pleasure, the mailing and wrapping was a chore, and I did not reprint the book any more after my mother died at the good age of ninety.

Still, it was not the end yet. My friend Lew Lancaster heard the story after he had decided to venture into publishing and offered to put out a new edition, this time in hard cover and illustrated. *The Blue Danube Cookbook* became an "officially" published book. I made few changes. The main

x

improvement was the changeover from ounces and pounds to cups and spoons primarily a painstaking labor of love by Jean Dehlinger, as well as additional recipes (as credited) and various clarifications by Lilly Oppenheimer, Trudy Lieser, Jane Politzer, Anita Schoonmaker, Emmy Sachs, and my wife Charlotte.

I added something too. Before I had the manuscript privately printed, I offered it to a publisher, drawing special attention to the title, which I thought particularly fitting. After he kept the manuscript for almost a year without responding, he eventually returned it, informing me of an unusual coincidence. He wrote that he too was planning to publish an Austrian Empire cookbook, and that he too had thought of the title *Blue Danube Cookbook*. (NOTE: Book titles are not protected by copyright.)

His book appeared soon afterward, faster than I could get my manuscript printed. But since I had submitted my title before his book was published, I am now adding the word "original" to my title.

It gives me great pleasure to acknowledge the emendations provided by my students in my Editorial Workshop at the University of California Extension. They delighted in picking out flaws in their instructor's manuscript.

And if you find flaws yourself, by all means help me in making the next edition better, please, and drop me a line. I will be grateful.

Berkeley, California, 1979

M.K.

xi

Conversion Table

ounces	grams	ounces	grams
1	28.35	9	255.1
2	56.7	10	283.4
3	85.0	11	311.7
4	113.4	12	340.0
5	141.7	13	368.4
6	170.0	14	396.8
7	198.4	15	425.2
8	226.8	16	453.6

Some frequent conversions

WHITE FLOUR:
16 tablespoons = 1 level cup = 120 - 130 g

GRANULATED SUGAR:
16 tablespoons = 1 level cup = 200 g

BUTTER, 1 cube:
8 tablespoons = ½ cup = 113 g

WALNUTS, shelled:
1 level cup = 100 g

NOTE: *All measurements for recipes in this book are designed for four to six servings unless indicated otherwise.*

Soups

Soups may be either thick or clear (bouillon).

Thick soups are prepared with "bechamel" or with thickening; all vegetable and legume soups are of this type.

Clear soups are prepared by boiling beef or beef bones; or chicken, duck, goose parts, such as giblets, necks, wings; or simply with bouillon cubes. (See Beef Soup or Bouillon.)

If an especially strong soup is wanted (for example, for a sick person), put the meats and greens in cold water, bring to a boil, then reduce heat and simmer until the meat is tender. If your emphasis is on juicy meat, with the soup just a by-product, put the meat in water which is already boiling. *Use about 1½ cups of water for each person* (some of the water will boil away) and about *1½ lbs. of meat for four persons.* Add other ingredients as specified in recipe, and bones, if available.

When the soup is done, remove fat: either skim it off, or refrigerate soup and remove the fat disc.

Serve in cups clear, or with accessories in soup plates. If

beef meat is used, slice it when soup is finished, salt again, arrange in a pan with some soup just to cover, and reheat for serving. If other meats are used, serve them directly out of the soup or use them for a rice dish, using some of the soup instead of water. (If not enough soup is available, add 1 - 2 bouillon cubes to the water for the rice.)

Finely cut parsley or chives go well with any soup.

BECHAMEL (butter and flour) and
THICKENING (water and flour)

"Bechamel" *as used in this book* ("Einbrenn" in German, "roux" in French), is a mixture of melted hot butter (or fat) and flour, to which later a liquid is added. Melt, but do not brown, the butter (or fat) in a pan over medium heat; add the flour, stirring all the time for 1 - 2 minutes if light ("white") bechamel is called for or if nothing is specified in the recipe, and for 4 - 5 minutes if dark ("brown") bechamel is mentioned in the recipe. Use 1 tablespoon of butter (or fat) for 1 tablespoon of flour to thicken 1 cup of soup, or more if thicker soup is desired. Before adding the mixture to the soup, put 2 - 3 tablespoons, depending on the desired thickness, of broth or vegetable water or soup or milk or other liquid to the butter-flour mixture, still stirring constantly over the flame — additional 1 - 2 minutes for light bechamel, 2 - 3 minutes for dark bechamel.

"Thickening" means mixing flour with water or with another liquid.

Goulash Soup

1½-2 quarts water
½ lb. or more of stewing beef
1 medium size onion
1 small potato in cubes
1 heaping teaspoon paprika
1 teaspoon caraway seeds
¼ teaspoon pepper, or less
¼ teaspoon ginger
1 clove garlic or some garlic salt
2 tablespoons fat
2 tablespoons flour (optional)
salt

Cut the meat in small pieces (hazelnut size). Salt it well. Chop the onions and the clove of garlic, and fry in fat until yellow. Add the meat and mix with the spices. Let it cook slowly first in its own juice with the lid on; stir from time to time. When the juice is nearly gone, pour on hot water for desired amount of soup. Let cook until the meat cubes are nearly tender, usually about 1 - 1½ hours. Then add the potatoes and seasoning and let them cook with the soup for 10 more minutes. If thickening is desired, add flour mixed with some cold water, pour into the boiling soup, and let it cook 5 minutes longer. Add a small piece of butter to the soup. Available liver or veal kidney, cut in cubes and cooked 5 minutes with the soup, improves it; a boullion cube makes it stronger.

Beef Soup or Bouillon

1½-2 quarts water
1½ lbs. meat (e.g., beef
   shank)
1 medium onion
1-2 cloves garlic
1 small carrot
¼ celery root
¼-½ lb. beef bones
   small piece of cabbage

green celery leaves
1 small can mushrooms or
   ¼ lb. fresh ones
5-6 peppercorns
5-6 whole allspice
1 bay leaf
   salt to taste — less if
   chicken bouillon cubes
   (1-2) are used

Use boiling beef, brisket, lean short ribs, or chuck roast. In the same way, use the necks, wings, giblets of chicken, duck or goose, and, if necessary, bouillon cubes (Wyler's).

Use a sturdy pot with a close-fitting lid.

Let water boil, put in the well-salted meat and other ingredients. Let simmer 2-2½ hours until tender without being mushy. Take out meat and skim off fat.

Serve in cups or in bowls with croutons. These can be bought or made from toasted sweet French bread.

More substantial soup can be made by adding cooked rice, barley, noodles, tapioca. If cream of wheat (4 heaping teaspoons) is used, see page 11. Barley has to be cooked for at least an hour (starting by placing it in cold water), and rice 25-30 minutes; then add to the finished soup before serving.

Vegetable Soup, fine

1½-2 quarts water
Beef shank
1 lb. fresh vegetables:
   onions, carrots, celery,
   green string beans,
   half cabbage, fresh
   Italian beans (shell

   when in season),
1-2 small potatoes—
   all cut up
1 can hot tomato sauce
   salt to taste — less if
   chicken or beef cubes
   (1-2) are used

Boil beef until nearly done, cut from bone, add vegetables. Let boil until tender and add tomato sauce during last 5-7 minutes.

4

Vegetable Soup, plain

1½-2 quarts water
10 - 12 ozs. mixed vegetables,
    fresh or frozen
    bechamel (see page 2)

bouillon cubes or beef
    soup
parsley or chives
salt

Cut cleaned vegetables into small cubes (or use a box of frozen ones) and cook 10 - 15 minutes with bouillon cubes. Make a smooth bechamel of butter and flour and add to the hot soup while stirring; cook 5 minutes more. Serve with white-bread toast cut into small cubes.

Potato Soup

1½-2 quarts water
  1 - 2 medium-size potatoes
  celery greens
  1 small onion, chopped
    fine
¼ cup milk or cream
¼ teaspoon caraway seeds
¼ teaspoon marjoram

¼ teaspoon or less
  powdered ginger
1 small clove garlic or
  garlic salt
bechamel (see page 2)
parsley or chives
bouillon cubes
salt (sparse)

Peel and dice the potatoes, salt the water, add vegetables and spices, except the onion. Cook 15 minutes. Melt (but do not brown) the bechamel butter, add the chopped onion and flour, and, while cooking over medium heat, add, as the bechamel "liquid," cold milk, stirring continuously into a smooth (not lumpy) paste. Put the paste into the boiling soup, stirring continually, let cook slowly for another 5 minutes, keep stirring. Add finely chopped parsley or chives. For thicker soup mix flour with cold water and add to hot soup, stir, and let simmer 5 more minutes.

Asparagus Soup

1½-2 quarts water
  bechamel (see page 2)
1 tablespoon sugar
  pinch of pepper
  pinch of nutmeg

1 - 2 cubes of beef or
  chicken bouillon (or
  beef stock)
  parsley or chives
  salt (sparse)

Cut off and discard the tough ends, wash the asparagus, and cut it into small pieces. Cook the asparagus until it is barely tender, 5 - 10 minutes. Make a smooth bechamel of butter, flour, and cold water, and pour the mixture into the hot soup, stirring it well. Add sugar and spices, let cook a little longer. Add parsley or chives. Serve with croutons if desired.

For an extra fine touch, see cauliflower soup below (yolk and milk).

Cauliflower Soup

1½-2 quarts water
  small cauliflower
  bechamel (see page 2)
  pinch of pepper
  pinch of mace

1 - 2 tablespoons milk
1 - 2 bouillon cubes (or
  beef soup)
1 egg yolk
  parsley or chives
  salt

Clean cauliflower, separate into flowerettes, and cook in salted water 10 minutes. Take out the flowerettes and keep them warm. Make smooth bechamel with butter, flour, and cold water, and pour mixture into soup. Cook a little longer. Before serving, mix yolk with 1 - 2 tablespoons of milk and pour mixture into hot, but not boiling, soup, stirring to prevent curdling. Now put flowerettes back in soup, or place them on soup dish, ladling the hot soup over them.

Tomato Soup

1 lb. (3 medium-size)
    tomatoes
1 small onion
1 tablespoon sugar
    walnut-size piece butter

bechamel (see page 2)
parsley or chives
vinegar
salt and pepper to taste

Cook tomatoes over low flame with little water and a piece of onion until soft. Put through sieve and thicken with flour and water or bechamel. If flour and water are used, add a dollop of fresh butter to the soup. Salt, pepper. Serve with toast squares of white bread or some cooked rice.

Actually, tomato soup is usually good from the can; follow directions.

Fresh Green Pea Soup

1½-2 quarts water
2 lbs. fresh green shelled
    peas
bechamel (see page 2)
1 tablespoon sugar

2 - 3 cubes bouillon (or
    beef stock)
parsley or chives
salt (little, because of
    cubes)

Shell peas, cook 10 minutes in water with cubes or clear soup, add sugar and salt. Make smooth butter-flour-soup bechamel, let cook 5 minutes longer. Serve with croutons and chopped parsley. If frozen peas are used, sauté them first in a small amount of butter and parsley before adding the water.

7

Dry Pea Soup

1½-2 quarts water	¼-½ cube butter
1 cup dry yellow or	1 - 2 frankfurters
green peas	1 - 2 bouillon cubes (or
¼-½ cup flour with	beef stock)
½ cup water	¼ teaspoon pepper
	salt or garlic salt

Soak peas overnight, pour on as much water as soup is desired, let cook until mushy, put through a sieve. Thicken with water and flour. Cook 5 more minutes, add salt, pepper, and the frankfurters, cut in small slices. Stir all the time, as it burns easily. You may use croutons instead of frankfurters. If you have some stock from smoked ham or smoked tongue, use it for this soup. Before serving, add a dollop of butter.

Ragout Soup

1½-2 quarts water	bechamel (see page 2)
¼ lb. or more veal	1 egg yolk
¼ lb. shelled green peas	1 - 2 tablespoons milk or
half of a small cauli-	cream
flower or asparagus	parsley
cut in small pieces	salt

Cut the veal into small pieces. Cook these 15 - 20 minutes in their own juice with a teaspoon of butter and chopped parsley. Then pour on the amount of water needed for the soup and cook until veal is tender. Now mix in the bechamel made with flour and butter; it should be light yellow. The green peas and cauliflower or asparagus should be cooked separately and put in last. Bind with yolk and milk, but don't let boil.

This soup usually has bread dumplings as accessory (see page 13). These can be cooked separately 5 - 6 minutes in salted water or in the ready-made soup and placed on each individual soup plate. Use the water of the cooked vegetables to cook them; then add the whole liquid to the soup. Last add the yolk mixed with cream.

Oxtail Soup

1½-2 quarts water
½ lb. oxtails
  fresh vegetables, any
    kind, chopped
1 medium-size onion

1 heaping tablespoon
  barley
1 small can stewed tomatoes
  or 2 - 3 fresh tomatoes
1 clove garlic, mashed
  salt and pepper

Boil the oxtails an hour or longer with the barley. Then add the chopped vegetables, onion, tomatoes, and mashed garlic, and cook until the meat leaves the bone. Serve with or without the bones (2 - 2½ hours in all).

Mushroom Soup

1½-2 quarts water
¼ lb. mushrooms
  bechamel (see page 2)

1 teaspoon caraway seed
  parsley
  salt

Wash, peel, and slice mushrooms thin. Sauté them with "a hazelnut" (½ teaspoon) of butter, parsley, and caraway seed. Pour on water, stock, or bouillon cube and cook 10 or 15 minutes; then make and add the bechamel with butter and flour. Cook 10 minutes longer. For a more substantial soup, add a thin drop dough (see page 11) when finished, and let come to one rolling boil.

Tapioca Soup

Put 5 - 6 tablespoons of quick tapioca into a good beef soup and let it boil 5 minutes.

Barley Soup (Graupensuppe)

1½-2 quarts water
¼ cup barley
  bechamel (see page 2)
  bouillon cubes or stock

½ cup milk or ¼ cup
  cream
1 egg yolk
  parsley
  salt

Put barley in cool unsalted water or, better still, in stock from beef or veal bones until mushy; cook about an hour. Pass through a sieve if desired. Pour on the amount of liquid you need, and then salt. Make and add the bechamel and cook 2 minutes longer. If you have some liquid from cooked ham or other smoked meat, use ½ cup, but in this case use less salt. Before serving, mix the yolk with the milk and add to the hot, not boiling soup, while stirring.

Chicken Soup

1½-2 quarts water
one stewing chicken or
  chicken parts
1 small carrot
1 medium-size onion

some celery root or
  celery leaves
bay leaf, whole allspice,
  peppercorns
parsley or chives
  salt

Cook chicken and other ingredients until meat is tender (about 2 - 3 hours or less). Skim off fat and serve clear or with a soup accessory. The meat can be served directly out of the soup or with a white sauce. Keep the fine chicken fat for dumplings.

Carp Soup

1½-2 quarts water
  head and tail, milt or
    roe from carp, or both
1 carrot
  bechamel (see page 2)

1 - 2 bouillon cubes
1 small onion
  piece of celery root and
    leaves
  salt, pepper

Prepare the fish by removing gills from the head, but not the eyes. Cook the fish in one pot and the vegetables in another. When both of these are done, put them through a sieve and pour on the necessary liquid. Thicken with bechamel; add bouillon cubes, salt and pepper, and, if you have milt or roe, add them also and cook 5 minutes longer. Croutons may be served with the soup.

Soup Accessories

Cream of Wheat in the Soup
(Griessuppe)

The cream of wheat should be poured slowly into the clear boiling soup while stirring all the time, and allowed to simmer 5 - 10 minutes. Usually 4 tablespoons are about right for 1½ - 2 quarts of soup. To enrich the soup, take a small egg yolk mixed with 2 - 3 tablespoons of milk and pour into the hot, but not boiling, soup, while continuing to stir.

Rice in Beef Soup

Rice may be cooked in beef soup or put into the soup which is already cooked. 3 - 4 tablespoons are usually enough for 1½ - 2 quarts of soup, and if you are short of soup, cook the rice in salted water and then add it to the soup. You can serve grated Parmesan cheese separately with the soup.

Drop Dough (Tropfteig)

1 egg   ¼ - ½ cup flour   salt

Beat the egg with salt, mix in a teacup with the flour until smooth. The dough should have the consistency of thick pancake batter. Pour the batter through a little funnel, circulating it into the boiling soup. Bring soup to one rolling boil only. You can also pour by hand, circulating the batter.

"Fried Peas" (Gebackene Erbsen)

1 egg
¼ - ½ cup flour

some milk
oil or fat for frying
salt

Mix ingredients (except oil) in a teacup so that the mixture resembles thick pancake batter. Heat the fat and pour in the batter through a colander, pressing it through the holes with a wooden spoon. The batter will form "peas." Fry them golden brown, using low flame, as they burn easily. Then take them out quickly with a perforated skimmer spoon. Place on absorbent paper or napkin and serve separately with hot bouillon or tomato soup.

Omelet Croutons (Biscuitschöberl)

2 eggs, separated
2 heaping tablespoons flour

parsley or chives
salt

Beat the egg whites stiff; fold in the yolks, flour, salt, parsley, or chives. Spread the mixture on a small well-greased baking sheet or flat pan and bake until a knife comes out clean, but do not let the batter dry out. Cut in squares like croutons and serve on a separate dish with the hot soup.

Fridatten

1 egg
1 cup flour

milk
salt

Make thin pancakes. Roll each up tightly, cut into thin strips and cook in water. Serve in a separate dish. Do not cook them in the soup.

Liver Croutons (Leberschöberl)

Follow the preceding recipe (Fridatten), but add ¼ cup of grated liver to the batter.

Cream of Wheat Dumplings
(Griesknöderln)

½ cup cream of wheat   pinch of nutmeg
1 egg   parsley
2 tablespoons fat   salt
2 teaspoons flour

Cream fat and egg, and mix in other ingredients. Form small balls with a teaspoon. Do not let the dough rest. As soon as you have finished preparing the balls, put them in boiling salted water and let simmer about 10 minutes. Pour a ladleful of cold water into the salted water with the balls and let them stand near the pilot light about an hour, covered wih a lid. Before serving, put 1 - 2 dumplings on each plate and pour the hot soup over them.

Breadcrumb Dumplings (Bröselknöderln)

1 cup breadcrumbs   bitter almonds
1 - 2 tablespoons butter   (optional)
or fat   pinch of nutmeg
1 egg   parsley
    salt, pepper

Beat the butter until fluffy, add the egg, salt, spices, (bitter almonds) and as many crumbs as needed to form balls. Cook in salted water or soup about 5 minutes. These breadcrumb balls can also be served in the sauce of chicken à la king in a ragout dish. The fat saved from soup is best for these dumplings.

13

Liver Dumplings (Leberknödel)

¼ lb. liver or less
2 tablespoons fat
1 large egg
breadcrumbs
ground ginger to taste

1 - 2 grated bitter almonds
(optional)
parsley
salt, pepper

Stir the fat until creamy, add the egg and mix, then add the raw and scraped liver, and other ingredients. Use as many of the breadcrumbs as will be needed to make a rather soft dough. The dough expands in the soup. Shape the dough into balls. You may also scoop out the dough with a teaspoon dipped into hot soup, instead of forming balls. Put the balls into the boiling soup and let simmer about 5 - 6 minutes. The balls use up quite a bit of liquid, so that if you are short of soup, you may boil them in salted water instead. To make sure that the dough has the right consistency, put one ball in a little salted boiling water and cook it. If it holds its shape, it is right; if it falls apart, add more crumbs. The breadcrumbs are best when made of sweet French bread. Be sure to take crumbs; do not use soaked white bread.

Butter Dumplings (Butternockerln)

½ cube butter
1 egg, 1 yolk
¾ cup flour, scant

4 tablespoons milk
finely chopped parsley
salt

Beat the butter until fluffy, add egg, yolk, flour, milk, parsley, and salt. Beat the mixture with a wooden spoon until the dough leaves the spoon. With a teaspoon, dipping it into hot water each time, form little dumplings, place them in boiling salted water, lift them, let them cook until they float on the surface, and then an extra 1 - 2 minutes. Try one ball; if it is too soft, add flour, if too hard, add milk to the mixture. If you have enough soup, boil the dumplings in it.

Salads
AND
DRESSINGS

There are many varieties of salads. You can use almost any kind of vegetable or fruit, also potatoes and fish. The basic dressing for leaf or vegetable salad, French dressing, consists of oil, vinegar, sugar, and water. The proportions cannot be given exactly; your tongue must decide. Usually one takes twice as much oil as vinegar, but some kinds of vinegar need more water, others less. The dressing (see end of section on salads) should be mild but tart, and the salad moist but not swimming in the liquid. Leaf lettuce should be fresh, not wilted. It should be washed, but the water should not cling to the leaves. It is best to wrap the leaves in a clean cloth, and, if used later, to store them in the refrigerator. Add the dressing (see page 24) before serving, and toss the leaves in it. Of course the lettuce needs salt. The use of mayonnaise is a matter of taste.

Fruit Salads

There are many tasty and attractive combinations of 2 or 3 fruits arranged on a bed of lettuce with various dressings. A sliced avocado combines well with orange or grapefruit wedges. Strawberries and melon balls go well together. Bananas combine with oranges and crushed pineapple for a dessert mixture without lettuce.

Juice from drained fruits should be used to combine with mayonnaise or boiled dressing.

Jello Fruit Salad

one 3-oz. package lime or lemon jello
two 3-oz. packages of cream cheese
1½ tablespoons sugar

one 8-oz. can crushed pineapple (save the syrup)
lettuce
1½ tablespoons mayonnaise

Pour 2 cups of hot water over the jello powder and mix well. When liquid begins to congeal, add the 2 small packages of cheese and the sugar, and beat with the eggbeater. Then mix in the crushed pineapple by hand, reserving the juice. Fill small cups and store in the refrigerator. After a few hours, or the next day, turn each cup out onto a lettuce leaf, and serve with a sauce made of the pineapple juice and mayonnaise blended together. Pour a little over each salad cup, and serve the rest separately in a sauce boat. Makes four ½ - cup delicious servings.

Vegetable Salads

Asparagus Salad No. 1

Cut and wash asparagus as for soup, discarding woody ends. Leave the stalks long. Cook in a small amount of salted water, drain, cool, and put the prepared dressing on it, with some pepper on top, and if desired, some mayonnaise.

Asparagus Salad No. 2 (with tomatoes)

Prepare and cook asparagus as for No. 1. Arrange tomato slices and stalks of asparagus on a lettuce leaf on individual plates. Put a little mayonnaise on top. If you use canned asparagus, marinate it in French dressing to give it more zest. No further cooking is needed for canned asparagus, but it should be drained well. This is an attractive first course.

Cauliflower Salad

Clean cauliflower and separate into flowerettes as for soup. Cook in salted water until soft but not mushy. Drain, pour the dressing over it, let cool, and sprinkle with pepper.

Potato Salad

This is the most common salad, yet it is often poorly prepared. Boil potatoes in their skins, and peel while still hot. Use a two-pronged fork so as not to break the potatoes. Slice or cube them, add salt, mix with finely chopped or grated onions. Add the dressing when the potatoes are still slightly warm, as it soaks in better. Cover the salad with the dressing to make it moist but not watery. Top with pepper or paprika. If you like mayonnaise, you may mix it with the dressing, but omit the oil. Add chopped parsley.

Cole Slaw or Cabbage Salad

Cut a fresh firm cabbage into quarters. Take out the core and shred the cabbage finely. Pour boiling water over it, and let it stand for an hour with a heavily weighted plate over it. If you want it softer, drain, and repeat the procedure. (Another way to soften the shredded cabbage is to place it over steam in your double boiler.) After draining, mix with French dressing; add some grated onion, pepper, a teaspoon of caraway seed, and mix well.

Bean Sprouts

Pick over the sprouts. Cover them with salted hot water, and let them stand ½ hour. Drain. Use any salad dressing, mixed with 1 teaspoon chive.

Beet Salad No. 1

Wash 2 bunches of beets and cut off tops. Leave ½ inch of the tops so that juice will not escape during the cooking. Cover with water and cook without salt for an hour or less. The time will depend upon the size of the beets. They will be done when you can easily pierce them through with a knife point. Put them in cold water, peel them like cooked potatoes, slice them thin, and add salt, sugar to taste, vinegar with a little water, a teaspoon of caraway seed, and a teaspoon of dried horseradish. If you can get fresh horseradish, peel and grate it, and mix it into the beets. (Fresh horseradish is hotter than dried, so use with care.) Mix well, and store in the refrigerator. The liquid should cover the beets. This keeps fresh a long time.

Beet Salad No. 2 (European style)

Proceed in the same way, but grate the beets after cooking, instead of slicing them. If you buy canned beets, which saves much time, improve them with caraway seeds, salt, sugar, vinegar (if necessary), and, of course, use the juice.

Butter Lettuce Salad

This is one of the finest salads. Take off the wilted leaves and the outer dark green ones. Wash and dry thoroughly. Add salt, mix well, and pour on French dressing; first oil (three parts), then a mixture of vinegar, water, and sugar (one part). Scatter chopped chives on top, and, as an extra luxury, decorate with quarters of hard-boiled egg.

Lettuce with Sour Cream

Prepare the same way as the above, but use sour cream as the dressing. Mix commercial sour cream with 2 - 3 teaspoons of vinegar and 2 - 3 level teaspoons of sugar, and pour over the salted lettuce, mixing gently. Neither oil nor other dressing is needed.

Cucumber Salad

Peel cucumbers and slice thin. Add salt and let stand for half an hour. Drain well, and mix with French dressing. For a crisper salad, do not let the cucumbers stand, but pour the dressing on at once. You may scatter some chives, pepper, or paprika on top.

Tomato Salad

Take firm tomatoes, and peel them if desired. To do this, either dip them in boiling water, or hold them over an open flame with a two-pronged fork. Chill for a while in refrigerator. When cold, slice them and add the dressing. Some finely chopped onion and chives are nice for flavor.

Green-bean Salad

Take the strings off fresh green beans, then cut them in 1-inch pieces or lengthwise. Cook in salted water, drain, and add the dressing. Scatter finely chopped onion and pepper on top.

Lima-bean Salad

Soak the dry beans overnight. Then cook them without salt, but do not overcook them as they should remain whole. Drain and add salt; add finely chopped onion, the dressing, and pepper.

Celery-root Salad

Take celery root only, but the smaller ones, because the large ones take longer to cook and are often hollow inside. They take about an hour to cook. When you can easily pierce them through with a knife point, they will be done. Cook them in their skin, and when done, hold them under the cold water tap. Scrape or peel the skin off, and then wash away the remaining skin particles. Slice as for potato salad, and add the dressing. Use pepper if desired.

Mixed French Salad

Boil 2 boxes of frozen mixed vegetables in a little salted water for about 10 minutes. Fresh vegetables also may be used. Add 1 large potato boiled in its skin, peeled, cooled, and cut into small cubes (like sugar cubes). Add 2 raw pippin apples, peeled and cored, and also cut into such small cubes. Add 2 or 3 pickled cucumbers, peeled if their skin is tough, and cut into small pieces. Add some anchovy paste or a couple of anchovy fillets from a can. Last of all, add mayonnaise to taste, mixed either with vinegar or a little of the vegetable water. Mix well, but gently; do not make a mushy salad. It should be moist, but not swim in liquids. Don't use either onions or garlic.

Fish, Shrimp, and Crab Salads

Fish Salad

left-over fish	*1 - 2 hard-boiled eggs*
2 - 3 cooked potatoes	*some capers*
a few pickles	*mayonnaise*
	lettuce

Remove all bones from fish and discard. Dice all ingredients together and mix with mayonnaise. Pile on dish, and surround with green leaves of lettuce. This salad is best when made with salmon.

Herring Salad

one 6-oz. jar herring snacks	*onions*
in sour cream	*1 stalk celery*
1 apple	*1 teaspoon sugar*
1 - 2 hard-boiled eggs	*lettuce*
lemon juice	

Buy the spiced luncheon herring snacks. Cut them fine, together with the onions in the jar and a few fresh onions. Add the eggs and apple, both finely chopped, lemon juice to taste, sugar, and a chopped stalk of celery. Serve on lettuce as a first course. (If you have used uncreamed snacks, add mayonnaise to the salad.)

Shrimp Salad No. 1

¾ lb. cooked shrimp
¼ cup diced celery
3 tablespoons salad oil
2 tablespoons lemon juice
1 tablespoon prepared
   mustard

1 tablespoon minced
   onion
mayonnaise or chili sauce
¼ teaspoon pepper
¼ teaspoon salt
some garlic salt
lettuce

Remove the veins from the shrimp. Mix all the other ingredients except the mayonnaise and chili sauce and pour over the shrimp. Cover and marinate 2 - 3 hours in the refrigerator. Serve in lettuce cups. Top with mayonnaise or with a teaspoon of chili sauce.

Shrimp Salad, No. 2

1 lb. cooked shrimp
5 hard-boiled eggs
4 - 5 tomatoes

lemon juice
a little grated onion
French mustard
mayonnaise

Dice the eggs and tomatoes, season to taste, and mix with the other ingredients. This is nice served in small glasses.

Shrimp Salad, No. 3

½ lb. cooked shrimp
green pepper
celery
green onions

tomato
olives
capers
mayonnaise
lettuce

Chop the 3 green vegetables fine, and mix with the shrimp and mayonnaise. Press into a teacup firmly, turn the cup out onto a small plate, and garnish with shredded lettuce. Decorate each individual salad before serving by placing a slice of tomato with 2 ripe olives, capers, or a shrimp on top.

Crab Salad No. 1

½ lb. cooked crab meat
2 small boiled potatoes
small pickles
mayonnaise

lemon slices
caviar
hard-boiled eggs
aspic

Cut the crab meat into small pieces and mix with diced potatoes, pickles, and mayonnaise. Garnish with lemon slices, caviar, wedges of hard-boiled egg, and, to make it more elaborate, with aspic. This salad can also be made with lobster.

Crab Salad No. 2

½ lb. crab meat
2 tomatoes
1 middle-size cucumber

green peas, cooked
mayonnaise
a little catsup
lettuce

Cut the crab meat and other ingredients into small pieces, and mix with mayonnaise. Surround with shredded green lettuce.

Dressings

Salad Dressing No. 1 (Italian)

½ pint mayonnaise
1 cup chopped olives
1 small green pepper,
    chopped fine

1 small can of red pimento,
    chopped fine
¼ cup catsup

Put all the ingredients into a bowl; mix well, then transfer to a jar and keep for future use.

Salad Dressing No. 2

½ pint oil
½ pint white vinegar
half a 14-oz. bottle of
    tomato catsup

½ cup mayonnaise
1 tablespoon paprika
1 - 2 cloves garlic
1 teaspoon salt

Mix all the ingredients except the garlic and put into a bottle. For a strong dressing peel the garlic, mash, and add to bottle. If you want dressing to have only a slight flavor of garlic, put *whole* cloves in, peeled but not mashed, and remove after a short while. Dressing keeps very long when stored in the refrigerator.

Fish
AND
SEAFOOD

Fish must be fresh. It is preferable to buy them alive, but if you cannot get them this way, you should examine them closely for freshness. The flesh should be firm, the gills reddish pink, and there should of course be no odor. Any fish can be made tasty, but my personal favorites are freshwater fish: carp, pike, salmon, and trout. When cooking, always use a low flame, and remember that the time will vary according to the size of the fish. Do not overcook.

Sautéed—An easy and delightful way to cook seafish is to sauté the fillets or steaks in olive oil. No breading is needed; simply sprinkle salt over the fish, place it in a pan in which olive oil had already been heated, and cook over a moderate flame until the fish is delicately browned on each side.

Broiled—Brush the fish and the broiler (or pan) with butter or oil; then add salt and pepper and broil 2 - 3 inches from 375° heat (3 - 4 minutes) until the fish is tender and cooked through. Baste frequently. Do not turn the fillets if they are thin and fragile, but if a whole fish is broiled, turn it once. Serve with tartar sauce.

Italian way—Any fish with few or no bones can be prepared this way. Heat a generous amount of parsley and a minced clove of garlic in 2 - 3 tablespoons of oil. Cook about 1 minute, then pour 1 or 2 6-ounce cans of tomato sauce (or freshly prepared sauce) into the pan and go on cooking for another 5 minutes. Put 2 lbs. seasoned fish fillets in this sauce, and cook gently with the lid on until done. Do not turn the fish as it is likely to break. A few leaves of celery chopped fine may be added to the parsley for flavor.

Fried—Salt, turn in flour, and fry the fish in hot oil or fat, using a heavy pan. If you like it breaded: salt, flour, dip in whole beaten egg, and then in breadcrumbs. Then fry on both sides. Serve with fresh salad or piquant sauce.

Baked Fillet of Sole

Choose a rectangular pyrex dish. Butter well and make alternate layers of fillets, seasoning them with salt, pepper, and bits of butter. Pour tomato sauce over the top of the fish, sprinkle some grated cheese over it, and bake at 350° about 40 minutes. Serve with a green salad.

Fried Carp

Carp is considered a delicacy in Austria and is therefore included here, although less readily available in this country.

If the fish is bought alive, allow ½ lb. per person; if it is bought killed and cleaned (without head or entrails), allow 6 ozs. Remove scales, head, and entrails, or have it done in the store. Divide the fish into 2- or 3-inch pieces, salt on both sides, and set aside for about an hour to let the salt soak in. Then dry on absorbent paper, and prepare to fry by breading. Fry slowly with the lid on; fish should not be raw inside. Carp is best from September to February.

Boiled Carp

Use 3 - 4 lbs. and clean or have cleaned. Cut in 3-inch pieces and salt well. Into a saucepan put water, 1 - 2 tablespoons vinegar, a bay leaf, 2 - 3 big onions (sliced), some peppercorns, some allspice, and a teaspoon of ground pepper. Let this come to a boil, plunge the well-salted, prepared fish pieces into the water, and simmer ¾ - 1 hour. Water should cover the fish by about 2 inches. When it is done, take it out with a perforated spoon, taking care not to break the pieces. Serve with browned butter and parsley potatoes.

Roasted Carp

Arrange the whole salted carp or the pieces in a roasting pan an hour before roasting on a half cube of butter. Break the other half cube over the fish in small bits. Roast in a 350° oven. If you like anchovy, mash some fillets with the butter, but use less salt. Brush frequently while the fish is in the oven. When done (45 minutes to an hour), take it out carefully onto a warm plate, dissolve the residue with 2 - 3 tablespoons of water, and pour it over the roasted fish.

Jellied Carp

Prepare the same as boiled carp, but use more sliced onions, less water. When done, arrange it on a deep china dish. Then mix the fish water with unflavored dissolved gelatin and pour it through a sieve over the fish. Store in the refrigerator.

Pike

A well-prepared pike is best roasted as a whole fish. To prepare it: scale and wash it, make incisions in the belly side, and salt it. Heat ½ cube of butter in a flat pan with a sliced onion and some chopped parsley, and arrange the fish on it. Spread breadcrumbs over the fish, put some more bits of butter on top, and roast it in a 350° oven, brushing it frequently with its own juice. This fish may also be prepared with some chopped anchovy fillets.

Salmon

In a deep pan put enough water to cover fish (whole or part) and add to it ¼ cup vinegar, 1 - 2 big onions, 6 peppercorns, 6 allspice, and salt. Heat water to the boiling point, add fish, and cook ¼-½ hour, depending upon the size of the fish. If you want to save the fish for later use, let it get cold in the water in which it was cooked. This helps to keep the flavor. Serve with brown butter or hollandaise sauce if warm, and with mayonnaise if cold; serve with vinegar and oil if preferred.

Salmon Slices

Use ¾-inch slices. Either buy them this way, or slice them yourself. Rub them with salt and pepper, and sprinkle them with some lemon juice. Put them aside for an hour. Then melt butter in a flat pan, and let the slices cook over a low flame about 5 - 10 minutes for each side. Serve the same as the salmon above.

Trout

These are best when caught in the mountains; if you are there, do not miss this treat; when frozen they lose much of their fine aroma. Trout should be cleaned of entrails, but not scaled. Cook them slowly in boiling water with ¼ cup vinegar and salt about 20 minutes; less if the fish is small. Serve with fresh melted butter. They may also be breaded and then browned in hot oil. Also they may just be baked in the oven. Sprinkle with bread crumbs, and put a piece of butter in the pan. Brush with their own juice.

Fried Shrimp (Prawns)

Boil 1 lb. large shrimp (prawns) about 15 minutes in water to which has been added: a large onion stuck with 1 - 2 whole cloves, a teaspoon of lemon juice, sprigs of parsley, salt, and pepper. Drain and then remove shells and black veins. Dip each shrimp in beaten egg and bread crumbs, and then fry in deep fat until golden. For serving, you can scoop out a large tomato and fill it with tartar sauce, or, if no tomato is at hand, put the sauce in a serving bowl. Serve on a round platter.

Fish or Prawns the Italian Way (fried or baked in batter)

Mix thoroughly 2 egg yolks and 4 tablespoons oil. Add salt, some flour, and a little water or beer to make a pliant paste. Beat 2 egg whites until stiff and mix into the batter. Now cover the fillets of fish or shelled, raw prawns with this mixture, and cook in hot oil on top of the stove or in the oven. Drain on absorbent paper when finished. Serve with mayonnaise or catsup.

Meats

The meat dish is the central part of a meal. It is the staff of life. Prepare it skillfully — lovingly.

When you buy beef watch the color of the fat — it should be cream-colored; the meat should be red and close-grained. The high-priced cuts — New York steak, T-bone steak, fillet steak, rib roast, and so on — can be prepared in a few minutes as steaks on top of the stove or under the broiler; as roasts, of course, they take longer.

The less expensive cuts — round "steak," Swiss "steak" (the word "steak" is misleading), cross rib, rump roast, and so on — can make excellent dishes. These cuts should be pounded, seared, slowly braised in their own juice, then water added gradually, and kept under a lid. They can be done on top of the stove but have to be watched so they will never be without liquid. If you have to watch TV — the meat requires slightly less attention when placed, with water, in a medium oven.

Pork should be rosy, the fat white, the meat finely grained;

31

lighter color assures you of a younger animal. Pork should be well done to eliminate vestiges of health hazards that may exist despite government inspection.

Veal must be very fresh and rosy, not wilted; it is particularly easily digested. A well-prepared veal roast as well as slices — either quick ("natural") in a skillet or breaded in hot fat — are delicacies.

In general: When you buy roasts, save the bones. Place them underneath the meat when you cook it; it is less likely to burn and makes better gravy. Take a pan according to the size of the roast; if the pan is too large the meat dries out. Fat meats (and fowl) should not be prepared with fat but with water. When the roast is done pour off the fat (saving it for later use) and serve the roast on a warm platter. Scrape the small meat particles clinging to the sides and bottom of the pan, pour on some water, add a walnut-size piece of butter, and let boil for a couple of minutes — this makes a fine natural gravy without flour. *Unless stated otherwise, the following meat recipes are prepared for 4 - 6 servings.*

Boiling Beef (Short Ribs) and Soup

3½-4 lbs. short ribs, brisket,	½ onion
or other boiling beef	1 clove of garlic
some beef bones	5 - 6 peppercorns
(optional)	5 - 6 allspice
several varieties of	1 bay leaf
available vegetables	salt to taste

Place all bones and vegetables in a pot of cold water. Rinse the meat briefly under running water. When the water boils, add the well-salted meat. Allow whole mixture to cook slowly about 2½ hours, testing after 2 hours to be sure that the meat does not become mushy. The time required depends on the amount and quality of the meat. Remove the meat from the liquid, and skim off excess liquid fat. This may be saved; it is especially good in liver or butter dumplings (see Soup Accessories). Serve the meat with a good sauce and vegetables or right out of the soup plate. It may also be sliced, salted again, and arranged in a pan with some chopped, transparent (fried) onions and then reheated with a little of the liquid. This liquid makes a delicious clear soup, whch may be served cold in summer, in cups, or hot in soup dishes with different accessories. When cooking the roast ribs, add additional beef bones to provide richer soup material for later use.

Roast Beef

Beef for roasting should be of top quality, otherwise it is better stewed. Either a roast with the bone in or a rolled roast may be used. For best results choose a roast no less than 4 - 5 pounds. Let the butcher loosen, but not cut off, the top fat crust, and tie it on again with twine before you roast it. Then you may lift it off and discard it when you are going to carve. (This will make the carving easier, and the juice will remain in the meat.) Season the meat with salt and pepper, and place it in a heavy pan with ¼ cup lard in a 450°-500° oven; reduce to 350° after 20 minutes. Roast it 20 - 30 minutes per pound, depending on the size and your preference, whether you want it rare, medium, or well done. Baste often with its own juice. When done, the meat should be served at once. The left-over meat makes delicious cold cuts. To make some gravy: take the roast out of the pan, pour off the fat, and loosen all brown particles from bottom and sides of the pan. Place pan over low heat, pour on ¼-½ cup water or bouillon, and simmer 5 minutes, stirring until smooth and not watery. Then add a piece of fresh butter. It is best to make a small amount of gravy.

Chuck Roast

This cut of beef may be boiled or braised. Sauté a large sliced onion, using a heavy pan and hot grease. Then pound, salt, and pepper a medium-size chuck roast, sear it on both sides, and let it cook slowly in its own juice with the lid on for about 10 minutes. When the amount of juice is reduced, pour on water, ¼ cup at a time, watching that the meat does not dry out or burn. This usually takes 2 - 3 hours. When done, there should be some short gravy left, which can be improved with a teaspoon of French mustard and a teaspoon of tomato paste. "Chuck roast" is made up of different kinds of meat in one piece. The "eye" is the best part and is often sold as "Jewish fillet"; the cooking time of this is shorter. If you buy the whole piece, you can easily take out the "eye" and use the other parts for ground meat, as it normally is stringy.

Braised Rib Roast Slices
(Rostbraten gedünstet)

A whole roast beef is often too much for a family. If so, buy slices, one for each person. Remove the fat, and make incisions in the edge of the meat to prevent it from curling. Pound the meat, rub pepper and garlic salt onto both sides, or use fresh garlic. Next fry a sliced medium-size onion in fat or oil in a frying pan until it is light yellow, and then place the meat in the pan. Sear on both sides. Cover and braise 1 - 1½ hours, adding water as necessary until done. Turn once or twice during cooking. The slices should be juicy and tender, and the gravy thick (not watery). Done this way, the meat will never be tough. As an alternative, put 2 - 3 tablespoons of sour cream into the pan to blend with the slices during the last 10 minutes. Stir frequently. Use no flour, or, at most, half a teaspoon for the natural gravy. Braising is a sure way to make meat tender. It can be done ahead of time and the meat can be reheated for serving.

Mock Fillet Roast
(Falscher Lungenbraten)

For this you may use the tougher cuts of meat such as round steak or Swiss steak. Buy at least 2 pounds in one piece and 3 - 4 inches thick. Take off all fat and skin, and lard with strips of bacon or salt pork (insert into the meat with a needle for this purpose). If you do not wish to go to such trouble, you may lay strips of bacon on top of the meat when you put it into the oven.

Start with a marinade of 2 parts vinegar, 3 parts water, 2 sliced onions, a bay leaf, peppercorns, a carrot, some celery, and some whole allspice. Boil this for 5 minutes and let it cool. Cover the meat with this cooled marinade, and keep it covered in an earthenware or china dish in a cool place or in the refrigerator for 3 - 5 days, turning the meat from time to time. Keep the marinade for later. When the meat is wanted for use, take it out, dry well, salt it, and place it in a pan with ½ cube of butter. Then put the meat in a well-heated oven (400°), and let it roast in its own juice for about ½ hour. When the meat liquid gets low, add some of the marinade to the pan. When the meat is nearly done, take it out of the pan, strain the sauce, and return sauce and meat to the pan; pour into the pan ½ cup of sour cream mixed with a heaping tablespoon of flour, 2 - 3 cubes of sugar, and some capers; no more vinegar is needed. Stir and baste frequently. This kind of meat takes about 2 - 2½ hours. Serve with rice, croquettes, or noodles.

Filet Mignon ("Beefsteak")

Buy one thick 7 - 8 oz. mignon steak for each person. Heat a walnut-size piece of fat in a frying pan. When this is smoking hot, put in the steak. Wait 3 minutes (you could use an egg-timer), then salt and pepper this side and turn it over. Cook another 3 minutes, and then salt and pepper the second side. Place the steak on a warm plate with a small piece of butter on top and some underneath the meat. This is a good dish to make when you are in a hurry, and it has an especially fine taste. You can make a little gravy by adding a bit of water to the pan. Serve with fried or mashed potatoes. It may also be served with a fried egg or browned onions on top. It is delicious when served slightly rare. This same method may be used for a rib steak (entrecote). For a variation you may serve the steak surrounded with cooked mushrooms; or after you take the steak out of the pan, pour 2 tablespoons of sherry into the pan, stir, and then pour over the meat.

Fillet Roast, Simple (Lungenbraten Natur)

Take a 3 - 4 pound uncut fillet roast (such as mignon steak), cut off any fat or skin, salt well, and lard symmetrically with bacon or salt pork (see Mock Fillet Roast). Place in a long pan with ½ cube of butter, and roast in its own juice in a 450° oven about 30 - 40 minutes, basting frequently. Serve in thin slices with any vegetable. This is the finest roast and is never tough.

Fillet Roast with Sour Cream (Lungenbraten mit Rahmsauce)

Take the same meat as for fillet roast, natural. If there is fat, take it off as well as the skin, and lard it with bacon strips. Place ½ cube of butter, a middle-size onion, some cut-up vegetables (carrots, parsnips, stalk of celery with leaves, or celery root), 2 bay leaves, 4 - 5 peppercorns, and 4 - 5 whole allspice in a pan. Let it get hot, place in it the salted meat with 2 tablespoons of vinegar and ½ cup of water. Roast in the oven at 450° and brush frequently with its own juice until nearly done. Remove the meat, put the juice and vegetables through a strainer, and return mixture to the pan. Mix a cup of sour cream with a heaping tablespoon of flour, ¼ cup capers, 2 - 3 cubes of sugar and put in the pan along with the meat. Add a little water (or vinegar) if the sauce is too thick, and cook another half hour, basting frequently. The sauce should look light brown, neither too thick nor too thin, and should taste sweet-sour. The whole roasting time might be about 1½ hours. Serve with croquettes (see page 67, potato dumplings (page 68), or macaroni. Cut meat into slices ¼-½ inch thick.

Viennese Beef Goulash with Gravy (Wiener Saftgulasch)

2 lbs. beef of good quality
2 medium-size onions
½ cup of fat
2 - 3 cloves of garlic
1 teaspoon caraway seeds

½ teaspoon marjoram
1 tablespoon tomato paste
1 teaspoon paprika
¼ teaspoon ground ginger

Cut the meat in large cubes; fry the chopped onions in the fat to a light brown, add the paprika, the well-salted meat, pressed cloves, the other spices, and the tomato paste or 2 - 3 raw tomatoes. Let the meat cook slowly in its own juice, covered with a lid. When the juice has simmered down enough to cover only half the meat, add water. Total cooking time is about 1½ - 2 hours. The gravy should not be watery, and thickening should not be necessary. Serve with peeled potatoes which have been cooked in salted water, or with butter dumplings (see page 14). (For Veal Goulash, see page 43).

37

Meat Loaf (Hackbraten)

2 lbs. meat (beef, pork, and veal mixed)	bread crumbs
1 - 2 whole eggs	generous amount of parsley
1 onion, finely chopped	pinch of ground ginger
1 French roll	1 clove minced garlic
	salt and pepper

Buy the three kinds of meat in equal parts. If you cannot get the veal, take at least the mixture of beef and pork. Soak the roll or a slice of white bread in water, and squeeze dry. If you grind the meat yourself, grind the bread with it, otherwise mash the roll fine with a broad knife. Mix all the ingredients and form a smooth loaf without creases. Roll in bread crumbs, put 1 - 2 slices of bacon on top, and bake in a 350°-400° oven with ¼ cup water in the pan, about ½-¾ hour. Pour off the fat, take the meat out, and, if desired, make a little gravy with ¼ cup water or soup. Cut slices and decorate with green peppers filled with cooked rice and slices of tomato. Another version: Before the loaf is quite done, pour ½ cup of sour cream mixed with a tablespoon of flour underneath the loaf in the pan, and finish baking. Stir and baste from time to time. The sauce should be light brown.

Pork Chops, Braised

Remove the fat from the edges of 6 - 8 pork chops. Cut it into small pieces, and melt a little of it in a pan. Pound the chops well. Salt each one, rubbing one side with salt, and the other with garlic clove or salt. Dip the chops in flour, and then sear them in the pan which contains the melted fat. Add 1 teaspoon of caraway seeds. Braise them slowly, covered, adding ½ cup water, and turning them from time to time. When done, skim off any fat, add ¼-½ cup of water if needed, and serve the chops in their own juice without any thickening. Cooking time is about an hour for good-quality meat.

Pork Chops, Simple, Braised

Remove the bones from 6 - 8 pork chops, leaving only a small rim of fat on them. Pound, salt, and dip them lightly in flour on both sides. Then sear them in about 2 tablespoons of oil. Pour on ½ cup water, and let them braise (covered) until tender. The gravy should be a nice brown. If there is too much fat, pour it off and add a small amount of soup or water, scraping up all the brown particles from the pan. Prepared in this way, the taste is quite different from that of chops above, prepared with spices.

Pork Shoulder

This is also a good buy and good meat. Prepare 2 - 2½ lbs. in the same way as pork roast; have the butcher saw through the bone for easier carving.

Pork Chops, Breaded

The preparation is the same as for Wiener Schnitzel (see below), but pork chops have to be pounded harder on both sides. I find they are better than the veal Schnitzel if the veal is not of the best quality. Fry 6 - 8 chops carefully in fat or oil over a low flame. Start with the lid on, turn when brown, and finish without the lid.

39

Pork Roast

Pork roast is the simplest roast to cook, and the most tasty. I prefer the center piece (2 - 2½ lbs.) with the low chops; although it seems expensive, it is the better buy, because the bones are fewer and lighter. Ask the butcher to cut into the roast, but not quite through it, between the ribs and also lengthwise. Salt outside and also between the ribs, then place in a long pan with a cup of water, 1 - 2 sliced cloves of garlic, and a teaspoon of caraway seeds. Roast at 400° for ½ hour, and then turn the oven down to 350°; the cooking takes about 1½ hours. When the fat is clear after roasting about an hour, pour it off, and add some more water for gravy. When the meat is done, remove it from the pan. Scrape the residue off the sides and bottom of the pan, and make a short (unthickened) gravy, by adding about ¼ cup water and heating.

Veal Roast

Veal, when bought, should be rosy (not red) and solid. The best cut for roasting is kidney roast. Buy 2½ - 3 lbs. I always order it with the kidney in, and also ask for 1 or 2 extra kidneys. The kidneys are embedded in fat; do not remove this as it is good to eat and makes the meat juicy. If you wish, you may remove a little of the fat from the extra kidney. Have the butcher cut the meat between every two ribs. Take the thin skin off the roast, and salt well on top and between the ribs. Pour 2 - 4 tablespoons hot fat over the meat, and place it in a preheated (350°-400°) oven. Add an extra ½ cube butter to the pan, and let the meat roast in its own juice. When the juice is somewhat reduced, pour ½ cup of water or soup near the meat, never on it, and baste frequently. The time will be about 1½ - 2 hours. When the roast is done, remove it, keeping it hot. Drain off the excess fat, leaving about 2 tablespoons in the pan. Scrape the sides and bottom of the pan, and add a little water to make some gravy. Be sure it is not too watery. Shoulder and leg of veal are drier, therefore wrap some bacon over the meat. A little paprika on top of the meat makes a nice crust. Carve with a sharp knife and serve hot.

Lamb and Mutton

Buy 3 - 4 lbs. of leg or shoulder meat. Young spring lamb is prepared in the oven like veal roast, but with the addition of 1 cup water at the beginning. Omit the butter or fat. Baste often. For older lamb or mutton, skin the meat completely and free it of all fat. Rub the meat with salt, put it in a pan with a cup of water, sprinkle a tablespoon of caraway seeds over it, and 1 - 2 slivered cloves of garlic or some garlic salt. Roast at 350°, about 2½ hours, depending on the tenderness of the meat. Baste frequently. After an hour of roasting, pour off the fat, add some more water, and, if more fat accumulates, pour it off again. Finish cooking, and serve with the natural gravy without any thickening. Serve piping hot. The serving dish and the plates should also be hot.

Wiener Schnitzel
(Breaded Veal Cutlets and Chops)

Have the butcher cut several individual chops or cutlets for you. Each piece should weigh at least ¼ lb. Do not rinse. Take off the skin, and pound very flat. Salt and flour both sides. Dip in beaten egg (do not dilute with water), then in bread crumbs of sweet French bread. Fry brown on one side in hot fat or oil, then turn and brown on the other side. Decorate with lemon wedges.

Veal Cutlets or Chops, Natural
(à la Holstein)

Select 4 - 6 individual chops or cutlets. Do not rinse them. Braise them tender in butter in a covered pan for about ½ hour. When finished, put a lettuce leaf on each plate with the cutlet on top. On one side you may put scrambled egg with Parmesan or other ground cheese or chive, and on the other side, chopped ham. This is very fancy and attractive.

Breast of Veal with Liver Dressing

Buy the thick part of the breast (about 3 lbs.), and ask the butcher to make a "pocket" in it. Prepare the dressing described under Roast Chicken, but buy 2 - 3 ozs. of additional liver, mince fine, and add to the bread. Salt the meat inside and out. Fill the pocket with the dressing, and sew it up or skewer it. Roast with 4 tablespoons of fat and ½ cube of butter at 350° for about 2 hours. Add paprika on top for color. After the first half hour of roasting, add some water, if needed, pouring it beside the meat but not on it. Since the preparation takes some time, it would be an advantage to do it in the morning, and to pour hot fat (¼ cup melted butter) over it to seal the meat. Then it could be roasted later in the day, adding a little butter to the pan. Make a short gravy with about 1 cup of water and a little flour, if desired.

If the dressing is made ahead of time, it should be chilled before stuffing the meat, and then refrigerated until it is to be roasted. (Otherwise danger of food poisoning.)

42

Veal Goulash

Heat 1 cube butter or fat in a heavy pan, and sauté 2 - 3 chopped onions golden yellow. Add 2 lbs. cubed shoulder of veal, salt, paprika, and some hot pepper, and simmer about 1 hour in its own juice with the lid on. When the juice is reduced, pour on some water, ¼ cup at a time, and when the meat is done (it should still be solid), take it out and set it aside. Next mix ¼ cup of cream with 1 tablespoon of flour until smooth, pour this into the meat juice, cook a little longer, add 1 teaspoon of vinegar and 1 teaspoon of tomato paste, and mix well. Return the meat to the pan, mix it with the sauce, reheat it and serve it hot. The goulash may also be prepared with a natural gravy, omitting the mixture of cream, vinegar, and tomato.

Lamb Shoulder Chops

Pound slightly and prepare in the same way as leg or shoulder, but cook covered on top of the stove, with ⅓ cup of water and no fat. Braise on one side; when nicely colored, turn and braise on the other side, again adding some water. I find this method to result in tastier meat than the broiling method, except for loin chops, which I find tastier when broiled. They will take about 1 hour. Loin chops need a hot broiler (350°-400°) and take 12 minutes altogether.

Breast of Lamb

Prepare the same way as shoulder, making sure to remove the fat. Breast is the most flavorful piece of lamb, but bony; therefore, count 4 - 5 ribs for each serving. Be sure, again, to serve piping hot on warm plates — the fat quickly congeals.

Field Hare, Natural

Field hare is popular in Continental Europe; in this country it will largely have to be replaced by domestic rabbit.

Use only the back and legs of the hare. Skin both completely and rub with pepper and salt. Lard, or wrap with strips of bacon or salted pork. Put the following ingredients in the pan — half on the bottom, the other half on top of the meat: ½ cube butter, a middle-size sliced onion, a carrot, a piece of celery, 4 - 5 peppercorns, 4 - 5 allspice, a bay leaf. Roast in a well-heated oven (350°) ½ to ¾ hour. Baste frequently, and you will get some good gravy, which you put through a strainer together with the vegetables.

Field Hare in Cream Sauce; Deer

Unlike in the United States, venison is freely obtainable in Austria, hence its preparation is included here.

A marinade is made of one part vinegar and two parts water and is cooked with the same vegetables and spices as above. Cook 5 minutes, cool, and pour over the meat, then store the meat in a cool place for 2 - 3 days, turning it from time to time. After marinading, proceed the same as with hare natural, but when you put the hare into the pan with the butter, use the vegetables from the marinade; no others are needed. Roast in a well-heated oven (350°) in its own juice. If necessary, pour on some of the marinade, and when half done, in about ½ to ¾ hour, strain the liquid which is in the pan, pour it over the meat, and add about 1 cup of sour cream mixed with a tablespoon of flour. Baste frequently and finish the roast, adding more strained marinade if necessary. Mix some capers and 2 - 3 cubes of sugar into the finished sauce, which should be light brown and taste piquant. Deer is done in the same way.

The "Little Meats"

Brains, Breaded

Use 1 lb. of beef, calf, pork, or lamb brains for 4 persons. Put them in cold water while you remove the fine membranes and wash off the blood. They have to be completely clean and dry. Cut them lengthwise, salt and bread them, using flour, egg, and bread crumbs. Then fry them in hot fat.

Brains with Eggs

Cook the cleaned brains in a tablespoon of butter and with chopped parsley, making them mushy with a wooden spoon: they should look white. Just before serving, add beaten eggs, mixing well while they cook. Add salt and pepper. The amount of eggs will depend upon the amount of brains; it should be brains with eggs and not eggs with brains. Do not overcook as they must remain soft.

Kidneys

Use only calf, lamb, or pork kidneys, 1 lb. for 4 persons. There is a very thin skin to be taken off. Put the kidneys into cold water, and let them soak half an hour or longer. Cut out the hard center part where the tubes originate. Fry some onions yellow. Mix in the kidneys, which have been sliced thin crosswise, sprinkle with a teaspoon of flour, and cook until they are no longer red, stirring all the time. Take them out onto a warm plate and add ¼ cup water to the residue to make a little gravy. Salt and pepper after cooking.

Liver

Buy 1 lb. of sliced liver for 4 persons. To prepare, pick off the thin skin at the edges. Fry ¼ chopped onion yellow, put in the slices which have been floured but not salted, and fry the liver quickly, first on one side, and then on the other. It should take no longer than 3 minutes in all, and, if slices are thin, even less. The meat should be rosy inside. Take it out of the pan and pour in a little water for gravy. Salt both the pan gravy and the liver when done.

Liver with Bread Crumbs

Do not pound. Proceed as with breaded veal, but do not salt until the cooking is finished. Use only baby beef or calf liver. Ordinary beef liver is usually tough, but it is all right for liver dumplings and stuffing, where it is minced.

Sweetbread (Kalbsbriese)

Sweetbread is considered a great delicacy; the best is from veal. Buy 2 pounds for 4 persons, rinse the blood off, and simmer in boiling, salted water 5 - 10 minutes. Let it cool. Rinse well in cold water, then with a sharp knife cut off fat, skin, and membranes. Slice the larger pieces horizontally in halves (through the meat, not between the sections) and let them dry in the refrigerator and with a paper towel. Then proceed in the same way as for Wiener Schnitzel; dip the slices first in (salted) flour, then in (two) beaten eggs, and finally in breadcrumbs. Fry in hot fat (Crisco, Snowdrift) until golden brown, about 3 minutes on each side, in a deep pan (electric is best). Serve with any salad or piquant sauce.

(This recipe and the next by courtesy of Lilly Oppenheim.)

Beuschel, Sour

1 beef lung	½ cube margarine
soup green	1 heaping tablespoon flour
1 medium onion	vinegar
1 - 2 bay leaves	

The lung together with the soup green, the bay leaves, and the onion (cut into quarters but not quite — the root end should remain intact) is put into cold salted water to barely cover. Cook covered 30 to 45 minutes; it is done when it has shrunk and has the feel of liver when pricked. Remove from broth, let cool. Prepare golden yellow bechamel. Cut the cooled meat into noodlelike strips. Strain broth and mix enough of it with the bechamel to make it possible to warm the meat strips in it with some sauce to spare. However, before adding the meat, add vinegar to taste. The dish is supposed to have a distinctly piquant flavor. It is customarily served with Bohemian Dumplings (see page 75).

Fresh Beef Tongue

First rinse well, and then cook a big raw beef tongue (2½-3 lbs.) in boiling salted water for 3 - 4 hours or less. Add a piece of onion and some peppercorns. When the meat is soft, put it under running water and peel. Small calf, pork, or lamb tongues are prepared in the same way, but they take less time. Cut the cooked meat into ¾-inch slices and serve hot; the little tongues should be sliced once, lengthwise. Serve hot with Polish sauce (best) or with horseradish. Cover the slices with some of the sauce. Serve with dumplings.

Smoked Tongue

Place a smoked tongue of about 2½ lbs. in plain hot water, cover with a lid and boil about 4 hours, adding hot water so that the tongue is always covered. After 1 hour taste the water, and if too salty pour the water off and replace it with fresh hot water. After another hour taste the water; if it is still very salty, pour it off again, replace as the first time, and continue to boil constantly. To see if the tongue is soft, pierce the tip, never the middle, to avoid loss of juice. The last water can be saved for later use. When the tongue is done, place it under running water 1 - 2 minutes; it will peel more easily. Begin at the tip and cut into slanting ¼-inch slices. Place in a pan, cover with some of the water in which it was cooked, and reheat. Mashed potatoes or mashed dry yellow-pea puree go well with it; it is best with creamed spinach. The last water may be used to cook barley or dry peas for soup.

47

Poultry and Game Birds

Roast Chicken

Buy a cleaned chicken; an average-size chicken serves 4 persons. Hold it under the running tap to rinse it inside and out, and singe it if necessary. Salt it inside and out, dry it, and brush it with salad oil. Place it in a pan in a 350° oven, with a walnut-size piece of butter and ½ cup of water. If young, it will take ½ - 1 hour, depending upon its size. When done take the chicken out of the pan. For gravy, scrape the brown particles off the sides and the bottom of the pan, add a little water or soup, and heat. The gravy should be short, not watery. Chicken may also be stuffed and roasted. It takes longer this way. Fill the chicken cavity with dressing (see page 52). Sew it up. Bake at 400° for the first 10 minutes, then at 350° until done.

Paprika Chicken

Divide the chicken into serving pieces. Chop a large onion and fry it in fat until yellow. Add a heaping teaspoon of paprika and the salted chicken parts; then cook covered until done — about 45 minutes. While cooking, add some soup or water, ¼ cup at a time, and a teaspoon of tomato paste; thicken with a teaspoon of flour and ¼-½ cup sour cream or top milk. Combine with the chicken juice and cook for another minute, stirring to prevent sticking.

Stewing Chicken (Suppenhuhn)

This is an older chicken and therefore takes longer to cook. Divide it into servings. Next take a sturdy pot and put into it some soup vegetables (carrots, celery), half an onion, peppercorns and a bay leaf. Add enough water to cover the meat. Bring this to a boil and then add the chicken parts. Turn low and let simmer for 2 - 3 hours. The chicken should be soft but not mushy. Serve with thin noodles (which have been cooked in the soup) in a deep soup plate; or serve the pieces covered with white sauce. The soup is nourishing and is recommended for sick persons. Take off the fat and use it in cooking.

Frying Chicken (Backhuhn)

Divide a cleaned chicken into quarters. Take off the skin; salt, shake in flour, then dip in beaten egg, then in bread crumbs from sweet French bread. Fry golden brown in fat or oil, using a deep pan. This is best when served with lettuce, cucumber or potato salad, and a juicy vegetable.

Turkey or Chicken Patties

Put slices of raw chicken or turkey through the meat grinder together with some sweet French bread which has been soaked in water and squeezed very dry. Add 1 - 2 eggs, ¼ or ½ cube butter, flavor with salt, pepper, parsley, and a pinch of ginger, form patties and fry them in butter like hamburgers. The same may be done with veal.

Chicken à la King (fine)
(Eingemachtes Huhn)

Divide a stewing chicken into serving pieces, and cook it in salted water with soup vegetables and half an onion. The cookng time will be 2 hours or longer. Next make a light bechamel with flour and butter, pour some of the soup onto it, and let it cook 1 minute. Then blend 1 teaspoon of lemon juice into it, add ¼ teaspoon pepper, and bind this sauce with an egg yolk and 1 tablespoon cream or top milk. The sauce should not boil any more after the yolk has been added; it is therefore advisable to blend it just before serving. Serve with flowerettes of cooked cauliflower, chopped parsley, and green peas mixed in the sauce. Cover the cooked chicken with the hot sauce, and serve the rest separately.

49

Roast Turkey

There is so much talk about turkey in the newspapers and magazines each Thanksgiving that I do not want to give it much space here. Suffice it to say that turkey is prepared like roast chicken but is rubbed with garlic salt inside. A turkey of average weight takes about 3 hours in a 350° oven. The dressing is the same as for chicken. If the liver is small, buy 1 - 2 ozs. more of any liver. Note that not only the cavity, but also the throat of the bird may be stuffed. You may use the same dressing or, for variety, a chestnut dressing.

Poulard (Pullet) and Capons

These are of the same family as chicken, only of finer taste and fatter. They are roasted like chicken, but without added butter, just brushed with oil for color. After an hour, when the fat is clear, pour it off and add some water sparingly. Finish roasting until nicely brown and soft. These are great and celebrated delicacies.

Roast Goose

Use a young goose, rinse it well inside and outside, and rub it with garlic salt. Put it in a deep pan with a cup of water, breast down, and put a teaspoon of caraway seeds on top. Roast in a 400° oven for half an hour, and then turn it down to 350°. After an hour, and when the fat is clear but not brown, pour it off and turn the bird over. The time of roasting depends upon the size and age of the bird. It may be from 1 - 3 hours. Prick the skin during cooking, so that all the fat will flow out and the skin will become crisp. Remove the goose from the pan. Scrape the sides of the pan for the delicious "scum," add a little water to it, cook 2 minutes, and make a natural gravy without any thickening.

Roast Duck

This is prepared the same way, but takes less time. A duck serves only 4 people, but to stretch it you can stuff it with the same dressing as is used for chicken; always use the liver for the dressing and a generous amount of chopped parsley: it will be delicious in the duck cavity. This is the simplest and, in my judgment, the best way to roast duck. Many of the variations described in newspapers merely spoil the wonderful flavor: it is barbaric to "improve" the duck with orange, cherries, and the like, as this only masks the true flavor.

Pheasants, Partridges

These may be roasted with a piece of butter like chicken, but should be larded with thin strips of salt pork or bacon. A partridge serves one, a pheasant serves 4 persons. When no larding needle is at hand, wrap the bird generously with whole bacon slices and tie them on with twine. Never use dressing for pheasants or partridge.

Dressings

Dressings should be moist but not wet, hence if eggs are large, take fewer than stated below. The dressing may be prepared the day before use and kept in the refrigerator, but should not be placed in the cavity of the bird beforehand.

Fine Bread Dressing

Use sweet French bread or toasted bread cubes from the store (but without the enclosed seasonings). Turkey will require about ¾ of a loaf. Soak the bread (preferably stale) in water, and squeeze it very dry. Put it through the meat grinder together with the liver from the bird and about 2 ozs. extra liver (not lamb). Add 3 - 4 whole eggs, mixing them in one by one, a generous amount of parsley, pepper, salt, a dash of nutmeg, ground ginger, 3 bitter ground almonds, and ¼ cube butter, melted (not brown) and cooled. Mix well until the dressing is fluffy.

Chestnut Dressing

Make an incision in the raw shells of about 20 - 30 chestnuts (not water chestnuts). Then roast them in the oven or boil them until soft, and remove the shells and brown skins. Cook them in milk until they are mushy, but they may remain lumpy. Add 1 - 2 tablespoons butter, pepper, and salt and fill the throat of a turkey loosely. This dressing should be moist; if it is too thick, add some milk. Sew up the skin of the throat with twine, and roast the bird as usual. Serve either separately or with the other dressing.

Eggs

Soft Boiled— These take about 3½ minutes in boiling water, depending on size. For accuracy use an egg timer. If you want the eggs cooked a little more firmly, put them in cold water and time the three minutes when the water begins to boil.

Hard Boiled— These take 10 minutes. To peel them easily, hold them a minute under cold water after boiling.

Fried— Do them in a little melted butter. If you want them covered with the white, put a lid on the pan.

Poached—If you want just one, place it in a small egg poacher, which is available in every hardware store. If you want more, cook them in slightly salted water in a skillet with 1 tablespoon vinegar and 1 quart water. Bring this to a boil and slowly slide in the broken eggs, one by one. The cooking time is 2 - 3 minutes. Take them out with a skimmer. They may be served with tomato sauce or hollandaise.

Eggs au Gratin— Poached eggs may also be used as a main dish. Take a fireproof dish, brush it generously with butter, and put the poached eggs into it. Pour ½ - ¾ cup of sour cream mixed with a teaspoon of flour and 2 tablespoons of tomato puree into it. Sprinkle some bread crumbs, grated cheese, and little bits of butter on top, and put the dish in a hot oven for about 5 minutes.

Scrambled—Sauté a little chopped onion in butter until transparent. Break the eggs into the pan and stir until creamy. Season with salt, paprika, pepper, or chive.

Egg Omelet—Break two eggs into a bowl, mix them, and add salt. Melt a tablespoon of butter in a flat frying pan, pour in the eggs, and shake the pan continuously to prevent sticking. Lift the edges of the omelet, tilting the pan so that the liquid can flow beneath the solid. Keep shaking the pan. When the omelet is creamy in the middle, roll it over onto a warm plate. Serve immediately. Do not use more eggs in a small pan; it is better to make several smaller omelets. An omelet may be filled with chopped ham, creamed spinach, or any leftover meat finely chopped and creamed.

Stuffed Eggs—Use any number of eggs, hard-boiled, and then plunged into cold water until completely cold for better peeling. Cut some of them lengthwise and some crosswise. Take out the yolks carefully, without breaking the white. Put the yolks through a sieve, or mash them with a fork. Whip ½ oz. butter for each egg, mix well with the yolks, add a pinch of anchovy paste, mustard, pepper, salt to taste, and, if too crumbly, add some oil, sour cream, or mayonnaise. Put the mixture back into the hollowed-out whites, either with a cake decorator or with a teaspoon. On top of each half: a caper, a small cooked shrimp, or parsley.

Herb Omelet— Beat together 4 whole eggs, 2 tablespoons milk, 1 tablespoon season-all, parsley, ¼ teaspoon pepper and ½ cup grated cheese. Pour into a hot buttered skillet, and fold over when set.

Fluffy Omelet—See Desserts.

Vegetables

Vegetables are important for nutrition. To save their valuable nutrients, they should be prepared with care, using as little water as possible. Leafy vegetables such as spinach should be cooked with no more water than that which clings to their leaves after washing — perhaps a trifle more if necessary; keep the lid on. Vegetables of the cabbage family should be blanched with boiling water and allowed to stand ½ hour with the lid on to make them more digestible. Then they should be cooked in salted boiling water; throw away the blanching water, but save the boiling water for use in soups or sauces. The water from spinach, however, is not good to save. Legumes (dry peas, beans, lentils) should not be salted while cooking, only afterward. Vegetables may be prepared either the "continental" way, with a fat-and-flour bechamel (see page 2), or a batter of water and flour; or the "English" way, using neither, but adding a walnut-size piece of butter and chopped parsley when done. Vegetables cooked in boiling water may be served with generously buttered bread crumbs.

55

Spinach

2 bunches spinach	pinch of ground ginger
2 tablespoons fat or butter	½ clove garlic or garlic salt
	some soup or milk
2 tablespoons flour	pepper, salt

English method— Pick the spinach over thoroughly; discard the wilted leaves and some of the stalks. Wash 2 - 3 times in warm water. Cook 10 minutes with the water that clings to the leaves, or very little more. Drain well, put through a sieve or chop, add salt and pepper; mix with fresh butter.

Continental method—Start as above. Then melt the butter or fat, blend in the flour, add soup or a little cream, and fold into the creamed spinach, adding the garlic and ginger. The bechamel should be thin and the spinach pulpy.

Carrots

2 bunches carrots	chopped parsley
2 - 4 tablespoons butter	peas, fresh or frozen
1 tablespoon flour	(optional)
1 teaspoon sugar	salt

Scrape or peel the carrots. Cut them in rounds or lengths of 1½ inches, or, when small, leave them whole. Melt the butter with the parsley, put in the carrots with water to cover, add the sugar and salt, and cook with the lid on. If you wish them to be creamy, mix the flour with water or clear soup, pour over the carrots, and cook one minute longer, stirring gently. They are usually mixed with green peas. If you use frozen peas, pour the thawed peas into the hot cooked carrots and cover with a lid to warm them.

Green or Wax Beans

Buy about 1 lb., remove the strings, and cook in salted water whole or cut in pieces. Serve with melted butter, or, if you prefer, with finely chopped onions or buttered bread crumbs on top.

Green Peas

Buy about 2 lbs. in pods; shell and wash them. Next melt butter with parsley, add the washed peas and 1 - 2 cubes sugar, a dash of water or soup, and salt, and cook until done. If desired, you can bind them with a teaspoon of flour in a little liquid.

Kohlrabi

Buy 6 - 8, peel off the hard skin, slice them thin, and cook them in water with salt and parsley, sugar to taste, pepper, and 2 tablespoons butter for ½ hour. If you want them creamy, thicken them with water and flour. They are often pulpy; if so, do not use them.

Asparagus

Buy 2 lbs.; peel them from the head down, cutting off the woody end pieces and all the "hangnails." Tie in bundles and cook in salted water, to which you have added 2 - 3 cubes of sugar, until slightly underdone. Drain and serve like cauliflower, or, if cold, with mayonnaise.

Cauliflower

Buy one head, then separate the cauliflower into flowerettes to make sure it is free of insects, which often hide inside. Cook until soft but not mushy in salted water, drain, and serve with melted butter and toasted bread crumbs or Hollandaise sauce. The cooking water and some flowerettes may be saved for soup.

57

Cauliflower au Gratin

1 cauliflower	*green peas (optional)*
bechamel (see page 2)	*chopped ham (optional)*
¾ cup milk	*grated cheese*
2 - 3 eggs, separated	*bread crumbs*
	some extra bits of butter

Boil the cauliflower until soft but not mushy in salted water. Place it in a buttered fireproof dish. Make a bechamel from the hot melted butter, the flour, and the cold milk, pouring on the latter gradually — the bechamel should be smooth. Let it cool a minute, then mix the bechamel with the yolks and the stiffly beaten whites into a batter. Add green peas and chopped ham to the batter if you want to enrich the dish, then pour the batter over the cauliflower. Top with bread crumbs and grated cheese, and add small bits of butter. Bake in a 400° oven until the dish is light brown on top. Take care not to let it dry out. Some milk may be added while the cauliflower is baking. Brussels sprouts and asparagus pieces may be prepared the same way.

Brussels Sprouts

Buy 1 lb.; take off the wilted leaves, and wash very thoroughly. Cook quickly until soft but not mushy; they should keep their color and shape. Serve either creamed or with melted butter and toasted bread crumbs.

Cabbage, Plain

Remove the outer leaves if wilted. Cut into quarters and boil in salted water about 10 minutes. Do not overcook; serve plain with meat or with buttered bread crumbs.

Red or Green Cabbage

1 firm cabbage	1 raw potato
½ onion	sugar to taste
1 tablespoon of fat, or	vinegar to taste
more	pepper
1 apple	salt

Take a firm head, red or green; discard the wilted leaves, and cut it into quarters. Remove the white core and shred the cabbage fine. Place it in a bowl, pour hot water over it, and press it down with a lid and a heavy weight. Let it stand this way half an hour or longer, then drain it. Next, place the cabbage in a saucepan in which you have fried half a chopped onion until golden. Stir, cover, and let it cook about 5 minutes in its own juice. Then cover with hot water and cook about half an hour. Add salt, sugar, and vinegar to taste. Grate a peeled tart apple and a raw peeled potato, mix with the cabbage, and cook about 5 - 10 minutes longer. Any excess liquid may be poured off or thickened. This should have a fine sweet-sour taste when done.

Curly Cabbage

1 solid head of cabbage	1 tablespoon fat
1 medium-sized potato	bouillon cubes or soup
½ teaspoon caraway seeds	minced garlic
1 tablespoon flour	pepper, salt

Wash and clean the cabbage conscientiously. Cut it into quarters, take out the core, and shred it fine. Pour on boiling water and let it stand ½ hour; then drain. Next put it in a saucepan with a raw, peeled, and cubed potato and the caraway seeds. Pour boiling water over it and cook 10 - 15 minutes. Drain off most of the water and thicken with a thin bechamel of the flour and fat, cooked light yellow; pour on some soup or water if necessary, and flavor with pepper, minced garlic, and 1 - 2 beef or chicken bouillon cubes.

Cabbage Rolls

1 cabbage	1 onion
1 lb. ground beef, mixed with pork and veal, if available	fat
	some soup

Cut off the cabbage leaves. Pour boiling water over them, and let them stand 30 minutes or longer. Drain, take two or three leaves together each time, and spread them with the meat mixture, prepared as for hamburgers. Roll the leaves together and fasten each roll with white thread or a toothpick. Sauté some onion in fat, put it in the bottom of a casserole, place the rolls in one by one, pour about half a cup of soup over them, and bake in a 350° oven 40 - 60 minutes. Do not forget to take out the toothpicks or remove the thread before serving. During the last 10 minutes you can pour one small can of tomato sauce over the rolls, if desired.

Sauerkraut

one 2-lb. can or jar of sauerkraut	1 medium-sized onion
1 sour apple	2 - 3 tablespoons fat
1 potato	2 - 3 tablespoons sugar

Place the sauerkraut in a deep saucepan. Cover with cold water about an inch over the contents, and cook with the lid on about 20 minutes. Then add a peeled and grated apple, a peeled and grated potato, and mix well. Chop the onion, fry until yellow, combine with the kraut, and cook 10 minutes longer, stirring constantly, and having also added the sugar to taste. It should look saucelike, neither dry nor too watery. Sauerkraut is especially nice served with smoked meat or frankfurters and as a side dish with potato dumplings. It can be reheated 2 - 3 times and always improves. If well prepared, it is delicious.

Romaine Lettuce

1 large or several small
    heads of Romaine
    lettuce
1 - 2 tablespoons flour
    some soup or vegetable
    water

2 tablespoons butter
green peas
pepper
salt

Use all leaves, not only the tender ones, but trim off
1 - 2 inches of the top and some of the coarse ribs. Wash the
lettuce and cook it 8 - 10 minutes with the water that clings
to the leaves and a trifle more. Drain and chop it coarsely.
Make a thin bechamel with some soup or vegetable water.
Fold in some thawed green peas, which need not be cooked,
only heated through with the cooked lettuce. This is a fine
vegetable if well prepared. If fresh peas are used, cook them
with the lettuce leaves.

Celery Root, Breaded

1 - 2 celery roots
1 - 2 whole eggs
    fat for frying

flour
bread crumbs
salt

Cook the roots, without peeling them, in boiling salted
water. They are done when they can be pierced easily. Scrape
off the skin, rinse them under running water, and cool. Cut
them into ½-inch slices. Beat the eggs, salt the slices; dip
them first into flour, then in the egg, and lastly in the crumbs.
Fry golden brown. They may be served as a first course or
for lunch with a piquant sauce or a leafy salad.

61

Onions

Cook medium-large white onions in boiling salted water until soft but not broken. Mix a little flour and cold water in a teacup until smooth, pour it into the hot onion liquid, and stir. Add 2 tablespoons of butter, some chopped parsley, pepper to taste, and cook 5 minutes longer.

Zucchini, Special (Kürbis)

Use the large kind, removing the seeds, or the small cucumber-shaped kind. Peel, cut into strips the length and thickness of a finger, salt, and cover with a plate and weight. Let stand 30 minutes or more, then squeeze out the water. Pour on some vinegar. Make a thin bechamel (flour and butter), and cook the zucchini in it. Do not let get too soft. Add a generous amount of finely chopped dill greens if they are in season; if these are not available, use 2 - 3 tablespoons of tomato sauce, but dill is better. Add sugar to taste. This dish should taste sweet-sour.

Stuffed Green Peppers

6 green peppers	1 small onion
1 lb. ground beef (better	parsley
if mixed with pork,	1 clove garlic
half and half)	tomato sauce
1 egg (optional)	salt

Mix the meats, egg, some chopped onion, parsley, garlic, and salt. Cut off the tops of the peppers, wash out the seeds with hot water, salt inside, and fill with the meat. Put the tops on again, arrange the stuffed peppers firmly in a deep dish, one by one, pour on a thick tomato sauce, and bake in a 350° oven 45 - 60 minutes. Serve with salted boiled potatoes or with cooked rice.

Stuffed Tomatoes

tomatoes   butter
ground beef   bread crumbs
grated cheese

Stuff like green peppers. Hollow out the tomatoes and mix the pulp with the meat. Butter a round dish, arrange the tomatoes in it, and top with grated cheese, some crumbs, and little bits of butter. Bake in a 350° oven about 30 minutes. Raw tomatoes also make a nice first course. Fill them with mixed salad, chill, and then place them on a lettuce leaf to serve.

Lecso

3 - 5 peppers   2 medium-sized onions
1 - 2 tablespoons fat   3 - 5 tomatoes
     salt

Chop the onions and let them get soft and yellow in the fat over a low flame. Cut the peppers into ¼-inch strips, removing the membranes, salt, and let simmer with the onions, covered, for 10 minutes. Break the tomatoes in pieces, add to the peppers, and cook for another 10 minutes without the lid. The liquid should be absorbed, but the vegetable should remain moist. Serve this Hungarian dish with meat.

Lentils, No. 1

1½ cups lentils   onions
bacon   salt

Pick over and wash the lentils, being sure to remove the little stones that look like lentils; add 1½ cups of cold unsalted water, and soak overnight. Cook in the same water, adding more as it is absorbed, and cook until soft but not mushy; test after 10 minutes. Drain if any water is left. Mix with fried cut-up bacon and bacon fat, and put browned chopped onions on top. Salt only now, but cautiously, because of the bacon.

Lentils, No. 2

1½ cups lentils   lemon
    gingerbread or ginger snaps   sugar

Cook as before, but do not drain. Add some grated dry gingerbread (Nuremberg lebkuchen, if you can get it, is best), ginger snaps, or honey cake. If these are not available, use fresh gingerbread and crumble it; this also serves as thickening. Add finely cut or grated lemon rind, some lemon juice, and sugar to taste. The gingerbread can be made from Dromedary Mix. This dish should be moist and taste sweet-sour.

White Dried Beans

Proceed as with Lentils No. 1. When soft, thicken with water and flour, salt, sugar, and vinegar to taste. Add a little piece of butter. They should taste sweet-sour.

White Rice, No. 1

1 cup rice   ½ onion
2 cups soup, or a bouillon   2 peppercorns
    cube dissolved in 2   2 whole cloves
    cups of water   2 - 3 tablespoons fat
                                   salt

Pick the rice over, but do not wash it. Put it into a deep pan, add salt, and pour either hot water and a beef cube or beef soup over it. Add an onion cut in half, first sticking into its flat surface the peppercorns and cloves, and let this come to a boil. Cover with a lid, turn the flame down low, and simmer 25 - 30 minutes. If you have the oven on, put the rice in. If you loosen the rice, do it with a fork so that it remains fluffy, never with a spoon. If you are not dieting, improve the rice with some chicken or bacon fat or a fatty soup; this will prevent it from becoming dry.

White Rice, No. 2

1 cup rice	Parmesan or other
3 - 4 tablespoons fat or oil	grated cheese
2 cups liquid	tomato juice
	salt

Put the fat or oil into a flat pan; then add rice enough to cover the bottom. Heat this until the rice gets transparent and light yellow. Remove and put this amount ino a deep pan; repeat till all the rice is done. Proceed now as in No. 1. For a change, the liquid can be tomato juice mixed with some water. Put Parmesan cheese on top when you are ready to serve the rice. If you want a whole meal, such as a lunch, first cook chicken parts and chicken livers, and then cook the rice in the chicken stock.

Brown Rice

Use the same method as for White Rice No. 1, but remember that brown rice requires more liquid and a longer boiling time. Consult the instructions on your package of rice.

Soup Macaroni

soup macaroni ("al-phabets")	parsley
	1 - 2 small cans mushrooms
soup or bouillon cubes	some fat

As a change from rice, use this side-dish. Arrange the alphabets in several separate layers on a cookie sheet, and toast them yellow in a slow oven; watch carefully because they burn easily. Then place the toasted alphabets in a pan, and proceed as you would with White Rice No. 1, using less liquid, pouring the hot liquid over them, and covering with a lid. Add at this time the parsley and the canned mushrooms with their liquid. Use about 2 cups of macaroni to 1½ cups of liquid. The alphabets should be rather rich and not dry and should have the consistency of rice; use fat or a fatty soup, and stir with a fork only.

Potatoes

Salt potatoes—Peel raw potatoes with a potato peeler. Boil them whole if small, or cut them in halves and cook them in salted water with a teaspoon of caraway seeds. Drain them well, and let them stand steaming a minute in the drained pot. Keep the lid on except for a crack. Shake. Serve hot.

Spring potatoes—Peel the raw potatoes with a peeler, or better still, scrape them with a knife; cook them in salted water. They take less time than older potatoes. When done, drain off the water and roll the potatoes in melted butter and chopped parsley. Serve them immediately. They are a delicacy; don't miss the short time when potatoes are new. They may also be served with cottage cheese.

Mashed potatoes—Cook several raw peeled potatoes, after first removing all the "eyes." Salt the water, which should just cover the potatoes. When soft, drain off all the water. Shake well in the pot, then mash them against the walls of the pot by pressing them with the back of a fork until completely smooth. The mashing may also be done through a sieve. Add hot milk, little by little, and a piece of butter, while beating the mixture vigorously to keep it fluffy. Taste, and salt if needed. Decorate with chopped onions which have been fried golden in butter. Keep the mixture hot all the time.

Baked potatoes—Brush several medium-size potatoes with butter or oil. Place them in a 400° oven about 40 minutes, and serve them piping hot with more fresh butter.

Paprika potatoes (Kartoffelgulasch)—Cut 1 lb. of raw peeled potatoes into ½-inch slices, crosswise. Melt some fat in a pan, fry some chopped onions golden, add a heaping teaspoon of paprika, and add the potato slices. Salt and cover, lifting them from time to time. Then pour on about a cup of hot water and cook until soft, but not until the potatoes fall apart — about 10 - 15 minutes. These are good with frankfurter or garlic sausages; add them whole or sliced and just heat them through.

Swiss potatoes or Potatoes au Gratin—Peel raw potatoes, cut them in ¼-inch slices, and place them in one layer in a buttered ovenproof dish. Salt and cover generously with grated cheese. Repeat the layers, ending with cheese, little bits of butter, and bread crumbs. Pour milk over this just below the top layer; bake at 350° until brown and the potatoes are done — at least 30 minutes.

Pommes frittes—Peel raw potatoes and cut them in strips of middle-finger size. Fry them in deep fat or oil until golden brown. Keep them hot, and salt them before serving, shaking them well. They should be prepared shortly before dinner.

Straw potatoes in nest form—Cut up sliced potatoes into noodle-like strips. Arrange the prepared potatoes in a form (deep-fry basket), filling it about half way, and fry golden brown in deep fat. First dip the form in hot fat, and then fill it with the potatoes; press them down with a ladle. These nests can be filled with green peas, diced carrots, spinach, or other vegetables. Serve as first course or garnish to a roast.

Croquettes (Potato dough baked in fat)

1 lb. potatoes	2 eggs	bread crumbs
½ cube butter	1 cup flour	frying fat
		salt

Boil the potatoes in their skins. Peel; when they are done and still hot, work them through a sieve. Let them get completely cold; then mix them with the butter or margarine, egg, and flour enough to make a pliable dough without creases and cracks. Form a roll of 2 - 3 inches in diameter, cut it into walnut-size pieces, and form it into balls. Dip these in flour, then in the second beaten egg, roll in bread crumbs, and fry in deep fat. They should be golden brown. Serve with any roast that has a natural or creamy gravy. The potatoes may also be boiled the day before, so that they can be easily grated cold the next day. NOTE: Instead of frying in hot fat, you can boil the balls in salted water 10 minutes, remove them with a perforated spoon, and roll them in prepared buttered bread crumbs. Keep them hot.

Potato Patties (Kartoffelpuffer)

3 - 4 potatoes   frying fat
1 egg   salt
1 - 2 tablespoons flour

Grate the peeled raw potatoes, mix in 1 egg and the flour. Salt well. Heat a flat pan, brush it generously with fat, and put in the mixture; flatten it into a thin layer. Brown it on one side, turn, and brown on the other side. Place on a warm dish, leaving the patties flat or rolling them up. They can be used as a side dish with meat or as a luncheon dish, accompanied by a small dish of applesauce. NOTE: The raw grated potatoes should be used at once, because they get watery if they remain standing. If that happens, drain off the water. The patties should be eaten while hot.

Potato Dumplings (Kartoffelknödel)

1½ lbs. potatoes   1 - 2 tablespoons fat
¾ cup cream of wheat   bread crumbs
½ cup flour   onions
1 egg   salt

Cook the potatoes in their skins, and peel them — if possible the day before they are needed. The next day grate them fine. If they are to be used the same day, let them get completely cold before they are grated, to prevent their getting rubbery; or grate them when they are piping hot, not lukewarm, and let them get cold before they are used. Make a nice pliable dough by mixing with the other ingredients; take enough flour so that the dough does not stick to your hands. Make a roll about 2½ inches in diameter, and cut 2 - 3-inch pieces from it. Form long or round dumplings, and plunge them in boiling, salted water for 15 - 20 minutes; when they sink to the bottom, lift them with a wooden spoon. To test whether the dumplings are done, try one: divide it with two forks. Take the dumplings out with a perforated spoon, drain well, and roll them in prepared toasted bread crumbs, or leave them bare but covered with fried onions and some hot fat.

Luncheon
AND
SIDEDISHES

Ham and Noodle Soufflé
(Schinkenfleckerl)

6 ozs. egg noodles
½ lb. chopped cooked ham
    or any smoked meat
3 eggs, separated and
    whites beaten

1 cube butter
1 cup sour cream
    bread crumbs
    Parmesan cheese
    salt

Cook the noodles in salted boiling water about 7 - 10 minutes. Drain, but do not blanche. Add the butter and all other ingredients except the bread crumbs, and mix well. Transfer to a well-greased Corning fireproof dish lined with bread crumbs, and bake in a 400° oven about ½ hour. Some more milk may be added while the soufflé is baking in the oven. If the eggs are separated and the whites beaten, it will make a fluffier dish. Some of the butter may be used for the baking. Spread Parmesan and dabs of butter on top before baking. Serve with a green salad.

Mushrooms in Shells
(Champignons in Muscheln)

1 tablespoon butter
mushrooms, canned or
*   ½-lb. fresh*
parsley

caraway seeds
2 - 3 eggs
pepper
salt

Empty the canned mushrooms into a saucepan along with the liquid in which they came; add the butter, chopped parsley, and caraway seed, and cook about 5 minutes until the liquid has simmered down. This may be done ahead of time, if you wish. Before serving, reheat and add eggs in proportion to the mushrooms; the dish should look like mushrooms with eggs, not like eggs with mushrooms. Mix well, salt to taste, and arrange in small china shells or real shells. Serve hot. If fresh mushrooms are used, cook them with a few drops of water until done; then proceed as described.

Bechamel Roulade

1 cube butter
1 cup flour (scant)
1⅓ cups milk
3 eggs, separated

3 heaping tablespoons
*   Parmesan or other*
*   hard cheese, grated*
filling: spinach, ham, or
*   mushrooms*

Make a smooth bechamel with cold milk (see page 2). Let it cool, add the yolks, the beaten egg whites, and the grated cheese. Spread on a well-buttered and well-dusted cookie sheet, and let brown in a moderate oven. Take out and fill generously with prepared creamed spinach or other filling, and roll up. Sprinkle some more grated cheese on top, and cut into 1-inch slices. Serve warm with green salad.

Cheese Soufflé, No. 1

½ lb. processed,   dash of pepper
    pasteurized cheese   ¾ teaspoon salt
½ cup milk   parsley
6 eggs, separated

Melt the cheese in a double boiler; add the milk gradually, stirring constantly until smooth. Add the seasonings. Remove from heat. Beat the yolks and slowly add them to the cheese sauce. Fold this mixture into the stiffly beaten egg whites, and mix well. Pour into a well-greased 9-inch skillet, or, better, into an oven-proof Pyrex dish or casserole, and bake in a 325° oven about 30 minutes. Serve with a leafy salad. This soufflé does not fall until cut.

Cheese Soufflé, No. 2

3 tablespoons butter   1 cup grated cheese
3 tablespoons flour   pepper
3 - 4 eggs, separated   salt
1 cup milk

Melt the butter, stir in the flour, and pour on the milk gradually. Add the yolks, the cheese, and fold in the beaten whites. Mix well and bake for 25 minutes in a 250° - 300° oven. Serve as above.

Spaghetti

Cook 1 lb. of spaghetti for 7 - 10 minutes in salted boiling water; lift several times with a wooden spoon. Drain well and mix with a piece of butter and, if desired, with grated cheese. Serve with tomato meat sauce.

The Sauce:

1 large onion
1 small stalk celery
1 - 2 cloves garlic
1 tablespoon chopped
     parsley
fat or oil
2 lbs. ground beef

4 small cans tomato sauce
     or two 6-oz. cans
     tomato paste diluted to
     creamy consistency
¼ teaspoon pepper
¼ teaspoon salt

Chop together the onion, celery, garlic, and parsley. Brown them in fat, add the beef, season, add the sauce or diluted paste, and simmer about one hour until well blended and the meat is done. Serve over cooked spaghetti with grated cheese. This quantity is enough for 10 people.

Hot Cheese Sandwiches

Generously butter slices of day-old white bread and cover them with grated cheese. Sprinkle them with paprika, and heat in a 300° oven until the cheese is melted. Serve hot.

Vegetable Sandwich

Mix fresh butter with chopped parsley and spread on day-old bread slices. Cover with cooked green peas, cooked green beans, sliced radishes, and/or tomatoes sliced fine. This is an open sandwich, and is served cold.

Hot Liver Sandwich

Butter bread slices, cover them generously with a fine liverwurst, and heat them in a hot oven.

Sausage Baskets (Wurst-Schüsserl)

Buy large slices of bologna and make sure that the skin around them is not broken. Put them in hot fat until they curl and look like small baskets. Keep them warm, and fill each one with something different: scrambled egg, cooked green peas, mashed potatoes, or anything which strikes your fancy. They make a nice first course or decorate a meat roast.

Mock Oysters (Falsche Austern)

1 brain	bread crumbs
anchovy paste	some butter

Clean any brain (beef, veal, lamb, or pork) by removing the fine net around it with your fingernails. Soak it in cold water so that all the blood comes out. Cook 5 - 10 minutes in salted water. Drain and cool. Line small shells, china or real, with anchovy butter. Slice the cooked brain lengthwise and arrange in the shells. On top of each shell distribute bread crumbs and small bits of anchovy butter, and bake to get them hot and the butter melted. They can be prepared ahead of time and heated when wanted. Anchovy butter is made from unsalted butter or unsalted margarine combined either with anchovy paste from a tube, or with mashed anchovies sold in a can. Mix well with a broad knife. This is a fine appetizer.

Cream-cheese Balls

Take 2 packages of cream cheese, make little balls by hand, and roll them in any of the following ingredients: finely chopped cooked ham, finely chopped cooked tongue, grated cheese, caviar, chives, or grated pumpernickel bread. A variety of such balls is a nice garnish to cold cuts and hors d'oeuvres. Serve at cocktail time.

73

Crackling Puffs (Grammel-Pogatscherln)

½ lb. flour	⅔ tablespoon wine or water
½ lb. cracklings	1 egg
2 - 3 tablespoons milk	paprika
or sour cream	caraway seeds
1 cake yeast	salt

Put the cracklings through the meat chopper, or chop fine, avoiding the hard pieces. Make a pliable dough from the flour, the cracklings, milk, the yeast (which has been soaked in lukewarm white wine or water), and part of a beaten egg. Let it rest 1½ hours on your board. Roll it out to a ½-inch thickness, and cut it with a round cookie cutter, brushing the rounds with the remaining egg; sprinkle them with paprika and caraway seeds, and bake in a 400° oven until the top is brown. If the cracklings are very greasy and the dough is soft enough, omit the milk.

Mosaic Cocktail Sandwich

½ lb. butter	some left-over roast
½ lb. American or Swiss	some ham and cold cuts
cheese	pickles
½ lb. bologna sausage	anchovy paste

Prepare the meats, cheeses, and pickles by cutting into very small pieces. Mix the above ingredients until very smooth and not dry. Buy a long narrow loaf of French bread. Hollow it out with a long knife and fill it tightly with the mixture, which has to be pliable. It is also convenient to cut the loaf in half for easier stuffing; when compactly filled, put the two cut sides together and store this way. Wrap the loaf with the mixture tightly in aluminum foil and put in the refrigerator overnight. For serving, cut the loaf into ¼-inch slices. This tasty cocktail dish may be prepared in advance and sliced when needed.

Bohemian Dumplings (Semmelknödel)

4 French rolls	*2 eggs*
butter or margarine	*milk*
2 cups flour	*salt*

Cut the rolls into small squares, toast; you may also buy the prepared cut squares, which are on the market as toasted bread cubes (take the ones without herbs). Soak the squares in melted butter or margarine and set aside. Meanwhile prepare the dough from the flour and eggs, taking as much milk as is needed to make it pliable, not hard. Beat vigorously by hand with a wooden spoon until the dough leaves the spoon and looks satiny. Now fold in the well-soaked bread cubes, and blend well until all the cubes are covered with dough. Let rest ½ hour, then form 2- to 3-inch dumplings with a ladle dipped in hot water, and cook in boiling salted water about 20 - 30 minutes, depending on the size of the dumplings. Take them out with a skimmer, cut them in 1-inch slices, and drizzle melted butter over them. Or form a long roll instead of individual dumplings; dip your palm in cold water to make the roll even and to prevent sticking. Cook in one piece; it should float in the water. Cut the roll in slices to serve. To find out whether the dough is cooked enough, pierce it with a skewer or a pointed knife: when it no longer shows the raw mixture, the dumplings are done.

Pastry Shells (Butterteig-Pasteten)

Make a flaky pastry dough as explained in Flaky Pastry Dough Strudel; it should be well rested. Roll out until ½-inch in thickness. Cut rounds with a 3 - 4-inch cookie cutter. Cut out half of the rounds a second time with a smaller cutter, leaving a ring about ½ inch wide. Set aside the small cut-out buttons. Brush the edges of the whole rounds with egg yolk, and place the cut-out rings on top of them. Do this carefully so that the yolk does not run over the edges. Also brush the tops of the rings and buttons. Bake them all in a 450°-500° oven, and watch that they do not burn. The buttons need less time; take them out earlier. They form the lid of the pastry shells.

One can use many different fillings, such as creamed spinach, green peas, mushrooms, creamed chicken, or a fine ragout. It takes some time to make the shells, but the dough and fillings can be made ahead of time, and, if necessary, the baking may be done too. Reheat before serving. A very fine and not so common entrée.

Cheese Cookies

Use equal amounts of flour, butter, cream cheese (depending on your needs, say 6 ounces) and add a third of this amount Parmesan cheese. Make a dough and let rest until the next day.

Flatten the dough, cut into cookies, and bake at 350° until brown (about 15 minutes). Serve warm.
(Courtesy of Emmy Sachs.)

76

Sauces

There are warm and cold sauces. Cold sauces are mostly based on mayonnaise, and they differ only by the various added ingredients. You can use store-bought mayonnaise, but the home-made is better, because it has no flour in it (see recipe below); the disadvantage of home-made mayonnaise made by hand is that it does not keep and must be used the same day. The cold sauces are good as dips for hors d'oeuvres, or for cold meat or fish. Warm sauces are mostly used for boiled beef. Precise amounts of ingredients are hard to tell — use your tongue; a little more or a little less of spices depends also, of course, on how much sauce you make.

Cold Sauces

Plain Mayonnaise

1 egg yolk	1 teaspoon vinegar or
1 teaspoon sugar	lemon juice
pepper	1 teaspoon prepared
salt	mustard
6 - 8 ozs. salad or olive oil	

Beat the egg yolk and the dry ingredients by hand or with your mixer at low speed. Slowly pour in the oil, drop by drop, stirring all the time until the sauce is thick and you have obtained the amount you want. Carefully add the vinegar or lemon juice, and, if you wish, the mustard. If the mayonnaise is too thick, add milk, some beef or vegetable broth, or more vinegar.

Mayonnaise can be made in a blender in one minute, and it keeps well.

Tartar sauce—Add to mayonnaise finely chopped pickles, parsley, a few capers, about ¼ teaspoon anchovy paste, some vinegar and French mustard, and mix well.

Sauce Aurora—Mix mayonnaise with tomato paste to color it; this is nice with cold meat or fish.

Sauce with chive—Mix mayonnaise with finely chopped chive and some pepper.

Horseradish Sauce

3 - 4 tart raw apples	1 teaspoon salt
2 - 3 tablespoons vinegar	1 tablespoon freshly grated
1 - 2 tablespoons sugar	horseradish root

Grate the peeled apples, mix with vinegar, sugar, salt, and then with the horseradish. If fresh horseradish is unobtainable, use the dehydrated kind soaked in a small amount of water. If canned horseradish is used, go easy on vinegar.

Sauce Remoulade

4 hard-boiled eggs, put
    through a strainer
1 raw egg yolk
1 tablespoon French
    mustard
1 tablespoon chopped
    parsley
1 small finely chopped
    pickeled cucumber

1 teaspoon sugar
4 - 6 tablespoons olive oil
1 tablespoon capers,
    chopped
1 teaspoon finely grated
    onion
1 teaspoon pepper
some lemon juice or
    vinegar

Mix all the ingredients very well together, and make the sauce fine and smooth. To make it more luxurious, add a tablespoon of caviar.

Cumberland Sauce

4 - 5 tablespoons currant
    jelly (or plum jam)
juice of an orange and
    some grated rind
juice of a lemon

1 teaspoon prepared
    mustard
1/4 teaspoon pepper
a small glass of port wine
pinch of ground ginger

Mix all the ingredients well together and serve with warm ham, venison, or cold meats in a small sauceboat. This sauce does not require cooking.

Warm Sauces (Savory)

Hollandaise Sauce (simple)

bechamel (see page 2)	soup stock
vinegar to taste	pinch of pepper
1 - 2 egg yolks	

Make a bechamel, very light colored, pour on beef or chicken stock, mix everything well over a low flame, or cook it in a double boiler. Flavor with vinegar and pepper, and then bind with the raw yolks. Do not cook any more after the yolks are added. Salt if necessary; you may add a pinch of nutmeg for flavor. If you serve this sauce with cauliflower or asparagus, use the water in which the vegetables were cooked.

Hollandaise Sauce (fine)

3 egg yolks	lemon juice
1 cube butter	pepper and salt

Put the yolks in a small pan with salt and pepper, and mix well. Place the pan in a double boiler and add the butter gradually in little pieces. Keep stirring until the butter is completely melted, and add a few drops of lemon juice.

Tomato Sauce

1 small onion	soup	vinegar
parsley	sugar	garlic
¼ cup oil or butter		pepper
	tomato purée or canned sauce	

Chop the onion with the parsley and fry in the oil or butter 5 minutes. Add the tomato purée, and make it creamy by adding soup or water; add the other ingredients to taste. If you use canned tomato sauce, no diluting is needed. Should you use raw tomatoes, at least 1 lb. is needed, and they should slowly cook at least 20 minutes; strain the sauce, and use thickening if the sauce is too thin.

Dill Sauce

bechamel (see page 2)   2 - 3 tablespoons chopped
soup   dill
vinegar   1 tablespoon cream
sugar   1 egg yolk

Prepare a dark yellow bechamel. Pour on cold soup to make it creamy, flavor it with vinegar, sugar, and salt to taste. Lastly, add the finely chopped fresh dill and the cream mixed with a raw yolk. Do not cook after the yolk has been added. The yolk is optional; you may use 1 tablespoon of sour cream instead.

Mushroom Sauce

¼ - ½ lb. mushrooms   bechamel (see page 2)
parsley   soup
1 teaspoon caraway seed   salt

Sauté the washed, peeled, and sliced fresh mushrooms in an extra teaspoon of butter with chopped parsley and caraway seed until nearly soft. If you do not want to peel the mushrooms, at least clean them with a brush. Make a dark-yellow bechamel, and pour on soup or water to make it creamy. Add the sautéed mushroom mixture, and cook 5 - 10 minutes longer. If canned mushrooms are used, go easy on salt. If dried mushrooms are used, wash them thoroughly, soak them, and cook them a little longer. For the liquid you may use the soaking water or that which comes with the canned mushrooms.

Anchovy Sauce

bechamel (see page 2)   2 anchovy fillets or paste
soup

Make a bechamel, pour on soup stock to make it creamy, and mix in the well-minced fillets or the equivalent in paste, and boil about 5 minutes. Paste and fillets are very salty; hence use either unsalted butter or unsalted margarine.

Horseradish Sauce with Milk

bechamel (see page 2)
1 cup milk
1 - 2 cubes sugar
salt

grated fresh or de-
hydrated horseradish
4 - 5 peeled, chopped
almonds

Make the bechamel, keeping it white; pour on the cold milk and boil until creamy. Add the sugar, salt, the horseradish, and the chopped almonds. Cook over a low flame or in a double boiler. For this sauce do not use the canned horseradish, because it is sour.

Horseradish sauce with soup—Prepare the same as above, but keep the bechamel brown, and pour on soup instead of milk or bechamel.

Onion Sauce

1 medium-size onion
1 cup soup

bechamel (see page 2)
salt

Chop the onion fine and boil in the soup about 10 minutes. Set aside. Make a brown bechamel, stir in the onion with the soup to make it creamy, and salt to taste. It is not necessary to strain the sauce; the little bits of onion make it tasty. Serve with boiled beef.

Polish Sauce
(with cooked tongue or fish)

½ cube butter
1 heaping tablespoon
flour
¼ - ½ cup ground ginger-
bread, gingersnaps,
or honey cake

¼ cup raisins
¼ cup skinless, slivered
almonds (no other
nuts)
vinegar to taste
some finely grated lemon
rind

Make a deep yellow bechamel with the butter and flour. Pour on the warm liquid from a cooked tongue or fish (such as carp), and make a smooth sauce without lumps. Add the other ingredients, and if it is too thick, more of the liquid. The sauce should taste sweet-sour. If prepared perfectly, it is delicious. Mix well and serve hot; pour some of the sauce over the hot sliced tongue or fish, and serve the rest in a sauce boat. The water from tongue is salty, so no additional salt will be needed.

White Sauce (medium thick)

2 tablespoons butter
2 tablespoons flour
1 cup milk

pepper
salt

Melt the butter over low heat (do not brown), add flour, and blend well. Gradually add the milk, stirring constantly until the mixture thickens. This is your bechamel. Now add seasonings. If you want a thicker sauce, double the recipe in flour and butter, but not in milk. If a richer sauce is desired, use cream instead of milk.

Cheese sauce—Prepare the same as white sauce, but add grated cheese to taste.

Warm Sauces (Sweet)

Wine Sauce (Chaudeau)

4 egg yolks
⅓ - 1 cup of sugar

1⅓ cups light white wine
piece of lemon rind

Place the yolks with the sugar and wine in a deep pan; the amount of sugar depends upon the wine. Put the pan in a water bath (or use a double boiler) and cook, stirring constantly, until the liquid is like thick custard and coats the spoon. If no alcohol is wanted, use the same amount of orange juice, mixed with the juice of 1 lemon. If you do not have enough yolks, use 1 teaspoon of flour. Serve hot with warm or cold puddings and sponge cakes.

Vanilla-cream Sauce (Custard)

2 - 3 egg yolks
1⅓ cups milk
1 teaspoon cornstarch

vanilla sugar or a few
drops of pure vanilla
extract

Proceed as above; cooking in a double boiler is a safe method; watch so it won't get dry.

Coffee-cream sauce—Use the same method as for vanilla-cream sauce, but use strong coffee instead of milk.

Nut-cream sauce—Make the same way as vanilla-cream sauce, but mix in any kind of grated nuts.

Chocolate Sauce

1 cup water (not milk)
6 ozs. bittersweet
  chocolate

no sugar, or to taste

Break the chocolate into small pieces and cook over a low flame or in a double boiler, stirring constantly until it is melted. Add drops of vanilla, if desired, but there is already a taste of it in the chocolate.

Desserts

When you plan a cake, consider the baking form. It should not be too small, because the mixture will run over, and it should not be too large, because the cake will be too low. Generally I would say, a cake of 6 eggs needs a pan (form) 8 - 9 inches in diameter.

Make the cake a day before use. It has to be perfectly cold when you do the icing; it also cuts better on the second day.

Grease the pan only on the bottom with butter, and dust with flour or bread crumbs; then the cake walls will not shrink.

The oven should always be preheated; the best place to bake is in the middle of the oven.

The cake is done when a wooden peg or a knitting needle comes out clean (or a toothpick).

When you have meringue on a cake, cutting is done more evenly with a hot knife. Clean the knife after each slice.

In many of the following recipes nuts are used. To blanch almonds, pour boiling water over them and slip off the skins.

Hazelnuts should be toasted in their skins and then rubbed between the palms until most of the covering comes off. Butter is salted unless stated otherwise.

Sacher Torte

5 ozs. semi-sweet choco-
    late or 4½ ribs of
    Ghirardelli (140 g)
¾ cup sugar
1 cup flour (120 g) scant
5 large egg yolks

5 egg whites, stiffly beaten,
    with a pinch of salt
1¼ cubes sweet butter
    (140 g)
preserves

Cream the butter, sugar, and yolks until fluffy. Add the melted lukewarm chocolate gradually, creaming all the time. Gently fold in the beaten whites along with the flour. Bake in a cake form in a 350° oven for about 40 minutes. Let stand in the form until cooled — preferably overnight. Spread a thin layer of jam over the torte, and then pour the icing over it.

Icing:

3 ozs. (90 g) semi-sweet
    chocolate

2 - 3 tablespoons of salad
    oil

Melt the chocolate or chips in a double boiler, and stir until all the lumps are gone. Then add the oil, a spoonful at a time, and stir constantly until you get a nice consistency to pour over the cake. If you want to make the cake richer, serve stiffly beaten heavy cream on the side.

Pischinger Torte

This is a typical Austrian cake and can be made only if you are able to obtain the wafers *(Oblaten)*. Fill 5 separate layers of wafers with the following chocolate cream.

Filling:

3½ ozs. *(100 g, 3½ ribs Ghirardelli) semi-sweet chocolate or one 6-oz. package of chocolate chips*
½ *cup (100 g) sugar*

1 *raw egg yolk*
4 ozs. *(120 g, 1 cup) hazelnuts, toasted, then ground*
1½ *cubes sweet butter or margarine*

Cream the butter, sugar, and yolk until very fluffy; add the melted or ground chocolate, mix well, and add the ground hazelnuts. Spread this mixture evenly on the *Oblaten* between each layer, leaving the surface of the top one bare. Put the cake in the refrigerator overnight with heavy weights covering the whole top, not just the center. Next day make the icing. Melt about 6 ounces of semi-sweet chocolate morsels in a double boiler, and mix with a wooden spoon until smooth. Pour on 5 tablespoons of salad oil (not olive oil), one tablespoon at a time, and keep stirring until you have the right consistency. Be sure you have no lumps. Pour on the cake evenly. Let it dry a few minutes. If your icing does not come out satisfactorily, spread some grated chocolate topping all over. After icing keep the cake in the refrigerator. When you are ready to cut it, warm a thin knife and make small slices about 1½ inches wide. This cake is rich. Make it 2-3 days ahead of time if you wish.

Chocolate Layer Cake
(Simple Chocolate Torte)

5 eggs, separated
¾ cup plus 1 teaspoon
   sugar (160 g)

1 cup ground chocolate
½ pint whipping cream

Beat the whites, gradually mix in the sugar, the yolks, and the chocolate powder. Put into two shallow 9-inch cake pans which have been greased and dusted, and bake about 30 minutes in a 350° oven; do not overbake. When cooled, spread one layer with half of the whipped cream mixed with more chocolate powder and put the second one on top. Leave the other half of the whipped cream white and use it for the top and sides; if desired spread with a cake decorator.

Unbaked Chocolate Cake

This cake consists of a combination of two mixtures.

First mixture:

½ lb. semi-sweet choco-
   late, softened (200 g)
1¾ cubes sweet butter
   (200 g)

1 cup sugar (200 g)
about 1 tablespoon of
   cognac or some other
   liqueur

Cream the butter, sugar, cooled chocolate, and cognac very well; this mixture must look lighter than chocolate color. Press it evenly into a round form 8 - 9 inches in diameter, and let it rest in the refrigerator until completely stiff. Now add the marzipan layer.

Second mixture:

1¼ cups sugar (250 g)
12 ozs. (350 g, 3 cups)
   hazelnuts, toasted, then ground

some lemon juice
¼ - ⅓ cup milk

Make a soft dough of these ingredients, pouring the milk on gradually, and mix very well together; add a few drops of lemon. This mixture, which should look like marzipan, is now evenly pressed onto the first (stiff) chocolate layer.

Now the cake is ready for the chocolate icing. Use the one described in Sacher Torte, first taking the cake out of the form. Return to the refrigerator. This is a delicacy, like a bon-bon, and should be cut in slices not larger than 1½ inches.

Chocolate Cake (fine)

5 egg whites
4 egg yolks
½ cup plus 2 tablespoons
  of sugar (120 g)

4 ozs. (120 g, 1 cup) hazelnuts or unblanched,
  toasted and then
  ground almonds
4 ozs. (120 g) semi-sweet
  chocolate

Into the stiffly beaten egg whites mix gently but thoroughly all the ingredients for the cake. Bake in a preheated 350° oven until a knife comes out clean. Let stand in the form until the next day; then remove and cut through horizontally. Next prepare the filling.

Filling:

¼ lb. sweet butter
½ cup of sugar (100 g)
1 egg yolk

2 - 3 tablespoons strong,
  cold coffee (instant
  coffee may be used)

Cream the butter well with the sugar and yolk; gradually add the liquid or coffee powder; mix well. Then fill evenly between the two layers.

Icing:

4 - 6 ozs. semi-sweet chocolate chips

4 - 5 tablespoons of salad oil

Melt the chocolate and stir until all lumps are gone. This is best done over hot water. Pour on the oil gradually, and stir after each addition. Mix until the icing looks satiny. If too thick, add oil but no water. Pour lukewarm over the cake, always tilting the cake to make the icing flow evenly. Icing running down should be lifted onto the cake. When it has dried a few minutes, decorate with hazelnuts or almonds.

Fine Coffee-cream Torte

6 - 7 egg whites with
    a pinch of salt
¾ cup sugar (150 g)
3 ozs. (90 g, ¾ cup) almonds,
    blanched, then ground

⅓ cup flour (40 g)
extra: toasted slivered
    almond

Beat the egg whites, fold in the sugar, almonds, and flour. Bake at 325°-350° in two 8 - 9 inch wax-paper-lined pans. When cool, fill with prepared vanilla pudding, using less milk than the recipe calls for, or with a thick custard. Cool this, and mix instant coffee and a half cube of well-whipped sweet butter into the custard. Fill between the cake layers and put some of the filling on the top and sides. Sprinkle toasted chopped or slivered almonds on the top and sides.

Orange Torte

6 egg yolks
⅔ cup sugar (140 g)
5 ozs. (140 g, 1 cup)
    almonds, blanched,
    then ground

2 heaping tablespoons
    bread crumbs *less*
4 egg whites beaten stiff
grated rind of 1 orange,
    and some juice

Cream the yolks with the sugar until thick and lemon-colored. Gradually add the orange juice and rind and the almonds. Fold in the beaten egg whites with the bread crumbs on top, and mix gently.

Bake at 350° about 40 minutes. Serve either with an icing or with wine sauce (chaudeau). To make the icing, mix 1 cup powdered sugar very well with the juice of 1 orange until you get the right consistency for spreading on the cake. The same recipe can be prepared in a steam-pudding form; it takes about 1 hour. If steamed in a double boiler, fill the boiler only ¾ full and have the form well closed. A safe way to prevent water from seeping into the form is to spread some butter thinly on the edge before putting on the lid. A very fine dessert. If icing is used on the baked torte, decorate with orange wedges and then pour on the icing.

Lightning Cake (Blitzkuchen)

2 whole eggs
1 egg yolk
½ cup sugar, generous
  (110 g)
¾ cup flour (110 g)

1 oz. (30 g, ¼ cup)
  blanched almonds (or
  other nuts), then
  chopped
1 cube butter
⅓ cup raisins (50 g)

Cream the eggs, yolk, and sugar for about 5 minutes. Add the melted lukewarm butter along with the flour, and mix well. Spread on a well-greased cookie sheet, 10x12 inches, distribute evenly, scatter almonds and raisins on top, and bake at 350° for 15 - 20 minutes. Cut into squares the size you want. This is a good cake to go with tea or coffee and can be quickly prepared.

Linzer Torte (brown)

1¼ cubes butter
5 ozs. (140 g, 1¼ cups)
  hazelnuts or almonds
  (unblanched), toasted
  then ground
2 raw egg yolks

¾ cup (140 g) sugar
¼ teaspoon cinnamon
¼ teaspoon powdered
  cloves
lemon rind
a tart preserve

1 hard-boiled, grated egg yolk

Make a pliable dough from all ingredients, except the preserve. Arrange ¾ of the mixture in a spring form. Spread the tart preserve over the top in a thin layer; roll the rest of the dough into ¼-inch or ¾-inch round noodles (ropes) and arrange them into a lattice-like pattern on top of the cake. Bake in a 350° oven about 40 minutes. When it comes out from the oven, sprinkle with vanilla-flavored sugar. To make the cake especially attractive, put a dab of preserve in each of the lattices (alternating a red preserve and a yellow preserve looks colorful) after baking.

This cake remains fresh several days.

Linzer Torte (yellow)

1 cube butter, scant
  (105 g)
½ cup sugar, scant (90 g)
  jam, preferably currant

1 cup flour, generous
  (150 g)
3 raw egg yolks
3 egg whites, beaten stiff

Mix the butter and sugar very well; slowly add the yolks and flour by the spoonful, making a nice dough. Bake in a 8- or 9- inch spring form in a 350° oven until light yellow. Remove from the oven. Spread a tart jam evenly over the whole surface; and on top of the jam spread the beaten egg whites, mixed with some more sugar and another spoonful of jam. Return to the oven and bake until the meringue is brown. This torte is easy to make.

Flat Yeast Plum Cake (Zwetschkenkuchen)

1½ cups flour, generous
  (200 g)
¼ cup sugar (50 g)
1 egg, 1 egg yolk
½ cube butter
1 cake yeast
½ cup milk

fresh Italian plums
  (or apricots)
extra sugar mixed with
  cinnamon
extra butter (preferably
  sweet) on top
¼ teaspoon salt in dough

Make a yeast dough from all the ingredients except the plums. Beat the dough well until satiny in texture, and let rise until double in bulk. Roll out ½-inch thick, and put in two 9-inch cake pans or on a large greased cookie sheet. Arrange the plums the following way: Cut them in half lengthwise but not quite through, so that they still hang together. Take out the pits. Cut the halves in quarters, again not quite through — the plums will look as if they were pleated. Place them directly next to each other on the dough with the inner side up, until the whole surface is covered. Sprinkle sugar mixed with cinnamon generously on top and dot with melted sweet butter. Let rise again about an hour and then bake in a 350° oven about 30 minutes until done. Best when served slightly warm and on the day it is baked.

Walnut Cake (Nusstorte)

9 medium eggs
1¼ cups (250 g) sugar
½ lb. (250 g, 2½ cups)
  walnuts, generous,
  first measured, then
  ground

4 level tablespoons of
  bread crumbs from
  sweet French bread
  grated lemon rind

Beat the yolks with the sugar until thick. Add the walnuts and the lemon rind, then the stiffly beaten whites with the bread crumbs on top of them, and fold in well. Bake in three 8½-inch well-buttered spring-form or slide-lift pans in a preheated 350° oven for 40 - 50 minutes.

The next day put the three layers of the cake together, spreading two layers with the filling, and icing on the third. This cake yields 12 slices. Decorate the icing with 12 half walnuts along the rim, one walnut for each slice.

Filling:

Use a package of vanilla pudding (mixed with only half of the milk), or make your own thick custard. Cool, and mix with a handful of ground walnuts, add sugar to taste, and fold in 2 extra whites beaten stiff. This is the original filling of this excellent cake.

Icing:

1 cup sifted powdered
  sugar
about 2 - 3 tablespoons
  hot water

¼ - ½ teaspoon rum
  flavoring

Mix well to the right consistency and pour over the filled cold cake. An easier, but still very fine alternative is to fill the cake with whipped cream, and use it also as a topping.

Sponge Cake (Biscuittorte)

4 eggs, separated
¾ cup sugar, scant (140 g)
* grated lemon rind and*
*   some drops of lemon*
*   juice*

baking powder (one
*   scant teaspoon)*
⅔ cup flour (80 g) (or half
*   ordinary flour and half*
*   potato flour)*
¼ teaspoon vanilla extract
* pinch of salt*

Beat the egg whites until stiff and salt. Cream the yolks with the sugar until thick; add the lemon rind and juice, slowly fold in the well-sifted flour with baking powder and stiff egg whites, and mix well. Bake in a preheated oven at 325°-350°, about an hour. On the next day slice horizontally into two layers and fill with the following mixture.

Filling:

1 cube sweet butter
1 cup walnuts, measured,
*   then ground*

⅓ cup hot milk
1 egg yolk
½ cup sugar (100 g)

Put the ground nuts into a small dish or cup. Pour the hot milk over them and let them stand about 10 minutes or longer. Cream the butter with the sugar and yolk until very fluffy, add the cooled walnut mixture, and mix well.

Icing:

Use the same powdered-sugar icing as for walnut cake. Decorate the same way with half walnuts.

Three-layer Sponge Cake

Make sponge cake dough as described above, and bake it in 3 equal layers until well done. Fill and put them together with the following filling.

Filling:

1½ cubes sweet butter
¾ cup granulated sugar,
    flavored with vanilla
2 cups milk (and a little
    extra)

1 tablespoon flour
    rum or rum extract
    candied fruit

Mix the butter and sugar until very fluffy; set this aside.

Mix 1 cup milk with the flour, heat the other cup to boiling point, and then pour into it the floured milk, stirring constantly. When thickened, remove from the heat. When cooled to lukewarm, gradually fold the milk broth into the butter mixture, a spoonful at a time. Brush each layer on one side with rum-flavored milk; spread the filling between each layer and distribute some glazed chopped fruit upon it. Put the layers together, and put a chocolate icing on top. This icing is the same as for Sacher Torte on page 86.

Meringue Cake (Eiweisstorte)

| 8 egg whites | a few drops vanilla |
| 2 cups sugar (400 g) | extract |

Beat the whites until foamy, gradually add the sugar and vanilla, and beat until it forms peaks. This yields 2 layers in 9-inch round pans. Line with wax paper, bake at 300° about 1 to 1¼ hours. Cool well and fill when you need the cake. The layers may be stored in a box and taken out for use when company drops in at short notice.

Filling:

2 cups whipping cream	instant coffee
1 cup crushed pineapple,	candied fruit or
well drained	strawberries

Beat the whipping cream, mix in the drained pineapple, spread between the layers and on the top and sides of the cake. Chill well — if you have time, many hours or overnight. Another version is to make one layer of the meringue mixture on wax paper with a rim and another layer also on wax paper lattice-like with your cake decorator. Bake the same as above. Fill the first layer with whipping cream mixed with instant coffee, put the baked lattice layer over the whipping cream, and decorate the open squares with candied fruit or with halves of fresh strawberries. You can, of course, make a smaller cake with fewer egg whites.

Ladyfinger Torte (Biskotentorte)

Cover the bottom of a round or oblong wax-paper-lined china or metal form with ladyfingers. On top of each layer spread any one of the following fillings. To prepare the fillings cream the ingredients and add the liquid gradually. In all, use 30 - 40 ladyfingers, making 3 layers. Put the cake in the refrigerator and cover with wax paper and a heavy weight. Next day turn out and top with ¼ pint beaten whipping cream (also on the sides). Decorate with glazed cherries.

Filling No. 1:

1 cube sweet butter
2 egg yolks
½ cup sugar, scant
1 cup almonds ground
   in their skins

3 - 4 bitter ground almonds
   or 3 - 4 drops almond
   extract
1 cup milk or less

Filling No. 2:

1 cube sweet butter
2 - 3 egg yolks
½ cup sugar

1 cup ground blanched
   almonds
1 small can crushed pine-
   apple with juice

Filling No. 3:

1 cube sweet butter
1 egg yolk
½ cup vanilla-flavored
   sugar

1 cup ground toasted
   hazelnuts
milk to moisten

Filling No. 4:

1 cube butter
1 egg yolk

½ cup sugar
½ cup strong coffee extract
   or instant coffee

Cream of Wheat Cake (Griestorte)

6 egg yolks	¾ cup cream of wheat
1 cup sugar (200 g)	(120 g)
grated rind of half a	6 egg whites beaten stiff
lemon and some juice	¼ teaspoon salt in the
	whites

2½ ozs. (70 g, ½ cup) almonds, blanched, then ground

Cream together the yolks and sugar until thick and pale. Add the lemon and almonds. Gently mix in the egg whites with the cream of wheat. Bake 40 minutes at 350° in a square pan 10x10 inches, which is greased and dusted on the bottom only. (If no square pan is available, use a 9½ x 2½ inch round one.) After baking, sprinkle with vanilla-flavored sugar. Serve with wine sauce or orange sauce. The cake can be served lukewarm or cold, but the sauce should be hot.

Balanced Cake (Gleichgewichtskuchen)

1¼ cubes butter	2 teaspoons baking powder
¾ cup sugar, scant (140 g)	sliced peaches or halves
3 large whole eggs	of apricots, about
1 cup plus 2 tablespoons	2 cups
of flour (140 g)	

Cream the butter with the sugar very well, and then add the whole eggs, one by one. Sift the flour 3 times with the baking powder, add this gradually, and go on beating until mixed and thick. Preheat the oven to 350°, grease and dust a spring form, and bake the mixture about 8 - 10 minutes. Then open the oven door, draw out the cake along with the oven rack, and quickly place the fresh or well-drained canned fruit gently onto the mixture, the pieces close together. Return to the oven. Finish baking, about an hour in all, (until a knife comes out clean). Sprinkle vanilla-flavored sugar on top of the cake when it comes out of the oven. Let it cool in the form. Always butter and dust the cake form at the bottom only; it makes the cake higher.

Cottage Cheese Cake (Topfentorte)

1¾ cups flour (210 g)
1¼ cubes butter
    some bread crumbs or
      spongecake crumbs

1 egg yolk
1 teaspoon sugar
    a few drops of lemon
      juice or rum
    salt if butter is sweet

Make a smooth dough, kneading gently on a pastry board. Put ⅔ of the mixture in a spring form or cake pan. Bake about 15 minutes at 350° and then fill evenly, first spreading a few bread crumbs or cake crumbs on the half baked cake to prevent sogginess.

press dough in large pan

Filling:

1 pint small curd cottage
    cheese
½ cup sugar (100 g)
2 egg yolks
    grated lemon rind

2 egg whites, beaten stiff
some chopped blanched
    almonds on top of
    filling (optional)

Sieve the cottage cheese ("baker's cheese" is best for this cake), mix with sugar, yolks, and lemon rind; lastly put in the beaten whites and mix well. After spreading this filling on the cake, make strips from the rest of the dough, and arrange them in a lattice-like pattern. Brush with egg white and finish baking at 350°, about 40 minutes altogether. Sprinkle vanilla-flavored sugar over the torte when it comes from the oven while still warm.

Lovely! Try small amount of crumbs instead of lattice as dough is crumbly

Carlsbad Shortcake (Mürbteig)

1½ cubes butter
⅓ cup sugar, generous
　(80 g)
6 hard-boiled egg yolks

2 cups flour, scant (240 g)
grated rind of ½ lemon
　and some lemon juice
2 medium-size tart apples
　(made into purée)

Cream the butter and sugar; then add the grated or sieved yolks, a spoonful at a time. Lastly mix in the flour, rind, and lemon juice. Make a smooth dough; let rest 1 hour or overnight. Divide the dough and bake in two 9-inch cake pans at 350° for about 20 minutes; after baking sprinkle vanilla-flavored sugar on top of the layers. When cooled, fill with apple purée and put the layers together as one cake. You can also make cookies from this dough. In that case, you roll the dough out to the desired thickness, cut it out, brush each cookie with egg white, and sprinkle some chopped almonds or nuts over each one.

Short Pastry

1¼ cups flour (170 g)
1 cube butter
½ cup sugar, scant (90 g)

1 egg yolk
some lemon rind, grated
apple purée

Make a pliable dough (work with your hands), divide equally, and bake 15 - 20 minutes at 350° in two 8-inch pans. When cooled, fill with apple purée sugared to taste. Put the two rounds together, and sugar the top with vanilla sugar. For a larger cake double the recipe and bake in larger pans. This pastry is mostly used for making open tarts which, when cold, are filled with fresh or cooked fruit, and covered with jelly or whipping cream.

The following two pies did not grow along the blue Danube. I learned them in the United States and liked them so much that I would like to "naturalize" them into Danubians and hence include them in this book.

Lemon Chiffon Pie

1 cup flour   ice water
⅓ cup shortening

Mix the flour and fat very well with a fork, using just enough water to hold the dough together in a ball. The better you work the fat into the flour, the better your crust will be. Put on a floured board, roll to the right thickness, and fit into a pie pan. Bake at 350° until the crust is light yellow. Cool, and then put in the filling.

Filling:

4 eggs, separated (4 yolks   juice of 1½ lemons (or
    and 4 whites)   to taste)
1 cup plus 2 tablespoons   a little lemon rind,
    sugar   grated
                            pinch of salt

Put two egg whites into one bowl and the other two egg whites into a second bowl. Cook the other ingredients — 4 egg yolks, 1 cup of sugar, lemon juice and rind — except the whites and the two tablespoons of sugar, in a double boiler until thick. Beat the whites in the first bowl stiff, and fold them into the cooled yolk mixture. Then beat the others along with the extra sugar to make the meringue. Fill the pie shell with the yolk mixture, and spread the meringue evenly over the top. Return to oven and let meringue brown.

Chocolate-nut Angel Pie

2 egg whites
½ cup granulated sugar

⅛ teaspoon cream of tartar
chopped nuts

Beat the egg whites stiff. Add the sugar and cream of tartar and beat until glossy. Line a well-buttered pie pan with this mixture. Sprinkle some chopped nuts over all. Bake in a 275° oven about an hour until brown and crisp. Cool the pie thoroughly.

Filling:

¾ cup semi-sweet choco-
late morsels
3 tablespoons hot water

1 teaspoon vanilla extract
1 cup whipped cream

Melt the chocolate in a double-boiler, stir in the water, and cook until slightly thickened. Add the vanilla, cool, and mix in the whipped cream. Turn into the meringue shell, and chill 2 - 3 hours before serving.

Drawn Apple Strudel

2 cups flour	1 egg
1 tablespoon salad oil	1 teaspoon sugar
1 teaspoon vinegar	1/4 teaspoon salt
1 cup or less of warm water	

Put the flour on a wooden board, making a wide well in the center for the other ingredients, which you will gradually mix in. Work with a knife or fork until you get a pliable dough which will at first stick to your hands. Clean your hands, and with the palm of the right hand work the dough out until it gets smooth and is no longer sticky. This will take about 15 - 30 minutes. Now form a ball, brush with oil or melted butter, and turn a deep warm bowl over the ball. Let rest at least half an hour and, if time allows, exchange the bowl with another warm one. Next spread a tablecloth on a large table (one you can walk around), dust it with flour, and place the ball in the middle. Roll the dough out lightly a few inches without pressing, then lift it up and away from the cloth, and with the back of both hands (the thumb inward) extend it, letting it glide back to the cloth as you keep walking around the table, and continuing from the center outward until you have a thin sheet. Cut off the narrow thick remaining rim with a sharp knife.

Filling:

1 cube butter	1 cup raisins
3/4 cup bread crumbs	3/4 cup sugar mixed with
4 - 5 lbs. apples, peeled	cinnamon to taste (150 g)
and thinly sliced	1/2 cup chopped nuts or
(pippins are best)	almonds (optional)

Melt the butter and spread it generously over the whole surface of the dough; then cover with the toasted, buttered bread crumbs, apples, raisins, sugar, and chopped nuts. By lifting the tablecloth on the two shorter sides, roll the dough inward just an inch, then lift the tablecloth on the long side, and roll the dough to the end, brushing it with butter and closing it at the end. Bend the roll into a U-shape and set it carefully onto the well-greased oven sheet with both hands, brush with melted butter, and bake in a preheated oven at 350°-400° about 40 - 50 minutes until it is brown and the apples are done.

Note: If you get holes in the dough while stretching it, it does not matter. Just leave them and begin on another side. It would be helpful if you could attend a demonstration the first time. Theory cannot always replace practice completely, especially when it comes to Strudel. The drawing is accomplished more easily by two people, but skilled cooks can do it alone. Do not get discouraged if you do not succeed the first time.

Flaky-pastry-dough Strudel (Butterteig-Strudel; Tiroler Strudel)

2½ cups flour, scant (280 g)	apple purée, jam, or
2 cubes butter	cottage cheese
1 egg	egg white
4 - 5 tablespoons milk	chopped nuts
1 teaspoon sugar	½ teaspoon salt

Put ¾ of the flour into a separate bowl, make a well in the middle, and add the milk, egg, sugar, and salt. Make a pliable dough of this (called in kitchen language "noodle dough"). Next roll slices of the butter in the remaining flour. Roll out the noodle dough into a rectangle form of the same length as your oven sheet, arrange the butter slices on it in a wide strip, and fold the sides and ends over them. Then tap the dough slightly 2 - 3 times with the rolling pin, and roll it. Fold once more. Let it rest again, preferably overnight, and repeat the procedure. When you have done the rolling and folding three times, place the dough on your oven sheet and fill it with apple purée, jam, or cottage cheese, filling it in a wide stripe. Fold over first the short, then the long sides, brush with egg white, spread a few chopped nuts on top, and bake in a 425°-500° oven about ten minutes; look in the oven, then turn down to 400°. Total baking time about ½ hour. This dessert is easier to make than a drawn apple Strudel.

Note: In the summer this dough should be made in a cool place. Between rolling it should rest in the refrigerator.

Flaky-dough Strudel with Yeast

First part:

1 cube butter	*1 teaspoon sugar*	*⅛ teaspoon salt*

Second part:

1 package yeast	*2 - 3 tablespoons milk*
1 egg	*pinch of salt*
1 teaspoon sugar	*2½ cups flour (300 g)*

Divide the flour unequally and put in two bowls. In the first put one cup flour, the butter, sugar, salt. Make a dough, set it aside. In the other make a well, add the yeast (dissolved in the warmed milk), and then the whole egg, sugar, and salt, and make another dough, which should look like a pliable noodle dough. Let rise about half an hour, then roll out and put the other (butter) dough in the center. Fold them together and roll out. Do this two more times so that you have done it three times altogether. Then cut the dough in half, roll out, and arrange one half on an oven sheet. Sprinkle some bread- or sponge-cake crumbs on top, fill with any desired filling (dry apple purée, prepared cottage cheese [see cottage cheese cake], or prepared poppy-seed filling) and cover with the second half of the dough. Let rise another half hour until light, and bake 40 - 50 minutes at 350°-400°. Cut in squares and sprinkle with sugar.

Note: This Strudel, made with yeast, should not be confused with the flaky pastry (or Tiroler) Strudel.

105

Sponge Roll (Biscuit Roulade)

5 eggs, separated	1 cup flour, scant (120 g)
2/3 cup sugar (140 g)	

Beat the egg whites stiff, fold in the yolks, flour, and sugar. Butter and dust well a rectangular oven sheet, and bake quickly in a 350°-400° oven. Roll in wax paper and cool. Unroll and fill with jam or whipped cream, to which you may add sugar and instant coffee. When you do the re-rolling, start from the long side. This is akin to the American jelly roll.

Nut Roll

4 eggs, separated	2/3 cup sugar, scant (120 g)
4 1/4 ozs. (120 g, 1 1/4 cups) walnuts, measured, then ground	1 heaping tablespoon flour or bread crumbs

Proceed as in Sponge Roll. When cool, fill with whipped cream or butter cream.

Chocolate Roll

5 egg whites	1 1/2 tablespoons flour
2 egg yolks	2 1/2 ozs. melted sweet
3 tablespoons sugar	chocolate

Proceed as in Sponge Roll, and fill with whipped cream or butter cream when cooled, or with jam when still warm. Make an icing if desired. This is a simple roll and is a good way to use up leftover egg whites.

Butter cream filling:

For butter cream you need about 2 cubes sweet butter, 1/2 cup sugar (or to taste), and a handful of ground nuts or some instant coffee.

Salzburger Nockerln

8 tablespoons milk (or
just enough to cover
the bottom of your
baking pan — large,
oblong)

¼ cube butter
5 egg whites
3 egg yolks
3 tablespoons sugar
1 heaping tablespoon flour

Turn on your oven to 350°. Put the milk and butter into the baking dish, set in the oven, and remove when the milk is hot and the butter is melted. Next beat the egg whites stiff; fold in the yolks, sugar, and flour, and mix gently and well. Then pour this mixture into the hot buttered milk. Bake for about 10 minutes just before serving. The surface of the dish should be a nice yellow, and the inside soft like a soufflé. Serve directly from the baking dish with a thin custard sauce as accompaniment.

"Rice in Milk" Pudding

1 quart milk
1 level cup white rice
½ cube butter

sugar to taste
1 teaspoon salt

Heat the milk and then pour the rinsed white rice into it. Add the butter, sugar, and salt. Cook either in a 250°-300° oven or over a very low flame, stirring constantly — it burns easily if the flame is too high. The rice should cook to a mushy consistency and be neither too dry nor too wet — just moist. It takes about 45 minutes. Top each serving with melted butter and with cinnamon mixed with sugar. This is excellent for children and is liked by adults too.

Strawberry Ice Meringue

1 lb. strawberries	1 egg white
1 cup sugar	½ pint whipping cream

Wash, hull, and beat the strawberries in a mixer until quite creamy. Slowly add the sugar and egg white, and beat the mixture until stiff, like meringue. Put in the freezing compartment of your refrigerator, preferably overnight. Serve in glasses, on glass plates, or in meringue shells; top with whipped cream. The same can be done with other berries.

Orange Dessert

4 oranges	1 cup and 2 tablespoons
6 egg yolks	sugar
2 whole eggs	whipped cream
juice of 1 lemon	glazed cherries

Cut the oranges in equal halves, press out the juice, taking care not to spoil the skins. Put the orange juice, the yolks, whole eggs, lemon juice, and sugar in a double boiler and cook until thick, stirring all the time. Fill the shells with the mixture, and decorate (when cold) with whipped cream and a glazed cherry. Serve cold on glass plates.

Rice Soufflé

1 pint milk	3 eggs, separated
1 cup white rice (120 g)	lemon rind, grated
½ cube butter	¼ cup raisins
½ cup sugar	1 teaspoon salt

Heat the milk, add the rinsed rice, butter, and salt, and cook over a low flame until you have a thick broth. Remove from the fire and cool. Fold in the yolks, lemon rind, raisins, and sugar. Let cool to lukewarm, fold in the beaten whites, and bake in a round greased Pyrex dish 15 - 30 minutes. It should be fluffy, not dry. Sometimes you have to add more milk while it is in the oven. If you have a closed pudding form, cook this dish in a double boiler. Serve warm with raspberry or chocolate sauce.

Filled Pancakes (Palatschinken)

1 cup flour	butter or fat for brush-
1 - 2 whole eggs	ing the pan
1 tablespoon sugar	pinch of salt
1 cup milk	

Make a smooth batter without lumps. Brush a small skillet with the butter or fat, let it get hot, and pour in the batter with a ladle. One ladleful for one pancake. Tilt the skillet, and fry the batter first on one side, and then on the other, without brushing the pan again. Slip each finished pancake onto a warm plate; fill and roll up before serving. The batter should be thinner than American pancake batter.

These are akin to the Southern traditional crêpes suzettes. Sweet filling below, but a savory filling may also be used (spinach, etc.).

Filling:

any smooth jam	bread crumbs mixed with
grated hazelnuts mixed	sugar and sprinkled
with sugar and a	with butter
little lemon juice	grated chocolate (for
	children)

Kaiserschmarrn

½ cup milk
1 heaping tablespoon
    sugar
2 eggs, separated

½ cup flour, scant
a little margarine or
    shortening

Make a batter by dissolving the sugar in milk, adding 2 egg yolks and flour. Stir and mix well. Fold in 2 egg whites beaten stiff. Melt a small amount of fat in a frying pan, pour in the batter and fry over medium heat until well set and the bottom is golden brown. Turn over and let the other side get golden brown. If desired, raisins may be added to the batter. Still in the frying pan, tear the "pancake" into small bits (use two utensils) and let brown some more. Serve with a little sugar sprinkled over it and with side dish of lingonberry preserves (or whole cranberry sauce).

Cream Pancakes

1½ cups milk
3 tablespoons flour
2 tablepsoons sugar
5 eggs, separated

½ cube butter
lemon rind, grated
vanilla sugar

Put the milk in a bowl, and add the flour, sugar, yolks, melted butter (lukewarm), and some lemon rind; mix well. Beat the whites stiff, and fold them into the mixture. Butter a flat pan, and proceed as with ordinary pancakes, but fry only on one side. Sprinkle the uncooked side with vanilla sugar. Roll up. This makes fourteen pancakes. Serve warm, without a filling.

Pancakes à la Crêpes Suzettes

Make batter as for filled pancakes. Fold them over, double, and then cut them in half (wedge-shaped). Make a mixture of the ingredients listed below; heat this, and dip the pancakes in it. Serve them very hot.

Dip:

juice of 1 lemon	1 liqueur glass Cognac
juice of 1 orange and	1 liqueur glass Curacao
some rind	(optional)
1 tablespoon sugar	1 cube sweet butter, melted

Fluffy Omelet

4 eggs, separated	lemon rind, grated,
1 extra egg yolk	or vanilla
(optional)	pinch of salt
1 tablespoon cream	2½ tablespoons butter
3 tablespoons sugar	

Beat the whites until stiff. Mix the other ingredients (except the butter) together, and beat with a fork until pale. Fold this mixture into the beaten whites until well blended. Melt the butter in an omelette pan; when sizzling hot, pour the mixture evenly and lift the outer edges. Cook on top of stove slowly and shake the omelette continually back and forth. It should remain creamy and not be overcooked. Fold onto a platter and serve plain or with any desired filling. This omelette may also be used as a luncheon dish, omitting the sugar and lemon rind or vanilla, and adding pepper.

Omelet Soufflé

6 eggs, separated	preserves
5 - 6 tablespoons sugar	vanilla sugar
3 tablespoons flour	pinch of salt in the whites
rum flavoring or grated	
lemon rind	

Beat the egg whites stiff, fold in the sugar, flour, and flavoring. Bake in a flat pan, which has been generously brushed with butter, spreading the mixture evenly, and baking in a preheated 350° oven until the surface is dark yellow. Do not bake dry. Fill with any preserve and fold together. Sprinkle vanilla sugar on top.

Choux Paste (Brandteig)

¾ cup water	⅓ tablespoon sugar
½ cube butter	2 - 3 eggs
½ cup flour, scant (75 g)	½ teaspoon salt

Heat the water and butter in a pan; when boiling, add the sifted flour. Stir briskly until the paste is smooth and leaves the sides of the pan. Remove from the flame and go on beating until all the lumps are gone. Add the sugar and allow to cool to lukewarm. Now add the eggs, one at a time, working them in with a wooden spoon until they are completely combined with the dough. From this dough you can make Cream Puffs, "Windbeutel," or eclairs.

Cream Puffs (Brandteig-Krapferl)

Prepare dough as for choux paste. Using two spoons, drop tablespoons of dough onto a buttered cookie sheet about 3 inches apart, brush them with egg, and let them stand ½ hour. Bake them in a 375° oven for 10 minutes, then reduce the temperature to 350° and bake another 15 - 20 minutes. Do not open the oven door during the first 10 minutes; they are likely to fall. When they come out of the oven, let them stand at room temperature out of any draught. Make an incision on the side and fill with whipped cream, vanilla cream, or any other cream you desire. Sprinkle vanilla sugar on top.

Cream Puffs, fried (Windbeutel, Eclairs)

The preparation is the same as above. Instead of baking in the oven, fry them in deep fat until golden brown; then roll them either in sugar or grated chocolate, and serve them with any fruit juice (raspberry is excellent). You can also open these on the side and fill them. Fried cream puffs in elongated shape are known as eclairs.

Sour Cream Muffins (Rahmdalkerln)

1 cup sour cream	butter for pan
1 cup flour	1 tablespoon sugar
4 egg yolks	preserves
4 egg whites, beaten stiff	

Blend all the ingredients. Brush a muffin pan with butter, pour 3 tablespoons of the mixture into each cup, bake, take out and turn over. Serve warm with preserves and sugar on top.

Simple Cake

3 eggs, separated	1/3 cup raisins
3 heaping tablespoons flour	1/3 cup blanched, then chopped, roasted almonds
3 tablespoons sugar	some lemon rinds, chopped or grated
1 tablespoon oil (not olive oil)	

Beat the whites stiff, fold in all the ingredients, and bake 25 - 30 minutes in a 350°-400° oven. Cut in squares. This cake goes well with ice cream. Bake on cookie sheet or in square pan.

Yeast Gugelhupf No. 1 (exquisite)

4½ cups flour (560 g)	2 whole eggs
1 cup milk, approximately	4 egg yolks
2 cakes yeast	¼ teaspoon nutmeg
1 cup sugar (200 g)	3 - 4 bitter almonds, chopped (optional)
1¾ cubes butter	grated lemon rind
	1 teaspoon salt

Put the flour into a large bowl. Make a well, put in the dry or fresh yeast, add ¼ cup lukewarm milk and a teaspoon of sugar, and let it all dissolve for 2 - 3 minutes. Melt the butter to lukewarm (do not let it brown), add it to the flour; gradually add the rest of the sugar, the lightly beaten eggs and yolks, all the dry ingredients, and the rest of the milk. Mix very well with a wooden spoon until the dough is satiny and pulls away from the bowl and spoon. Cover with a clean cloth and let rise in a warm place until double in bulk. This may take 1½ hours or longer. When sufficiently risen, put the dough on a floured board or floured cloth. Flatten it lightly with a rolling pin or with the palm of your hand to rectangular shape. Now you are ready for the filling.

Filling:

1½ cups baked, dried, and grated gingerbread or gingersnaps	½ cube butter, melted
	½ - ¾ cup chopped nuts
½ cup liquid honey	1 tablespoon cinnamon mixed with sugar

Spread the grated gingerbread evenly on the dough, then sprinkle the honey and melted butter, and add the cinnamon and sugar. Roll the dough carefully like a jelly roll, and then lift it into a well-greased and dusted deep-fluted ring mold ("Gugelhupf" form). It is important to grease the mold especially well so that the cake does not stick to the sides and the center tube when it is turned out. Let it rise again until the mold is full to the top. Bake it in a preheated 350°-400° oven about an hour. When it has cooled 10 minutes, remove Gugelhupf by carefully turning the mold upside down on a rack; sprinkle the cake generously with vanilla-flavored sugar. Serve when completely cooled, preferably the next day. The same cake can be made without the above filling. It is also delicious, though not as elaborate. If you wish to do it this way, mix into the dough a generous handful each of raisins and of blanched, slivered almonds. Put the dough directly into the form, and let it rise only once. Dust the form with fine bread crumbs instead of flour — it gives a nice color. After dusting arrange halves of peeled almonds on top in the curves of the mold; this is convenient for slicing.

Yeast Gugelhupf No. 2

1 cube butter	1½ cups raisins
½ cube margarine	2 cakes fresh or dry yeast
4 - 5 tablespoons sugar,	chopped blanched
or to taste	almonds or mixed peels
4 egg yolks	(candied fruits)
2 whole eggs	lemon rind, grated
3 cups flour (420 g)	rum flavoring
1 cup half-and-half	1 teaspoon salt

Make the yeast dough as shown in Gugelhupf No. 1. Put the dough directly into the well-greased mold, and let it rise until double in bulk — usually this fills the form. Bake in a 350°-400° oven about 50 - 60 minutes.

Baking Powder Gugelhupf No. 1

1 cube butter	1 cup milk or cream
¾ cup sugar (150 g)	grated rind of ½ lemon
2 whole eggs	and some juice
2 cups flour (250 g)	some raisins
1 tablespoon baking	rum and vanilla flavorings
powder	½ teaspoon salt

Cream the butter with the sugar; add the eggs. Sift the flour with the baking powder and add alternately with the milk. Mix in the other ingredients. Grease the form well and bake in a 350° oven for one hour.

Baking Powder Gugelhupf No. 2

1 cube butter	grated lemon rind and
3/4 cup sugar (150 g)	a few drops of lemon
4 eggs, separated	juice
1 cup cream or whole	some raisins
milk	rum and vanilla
2 cups flour, scant	flavorings
(250 g)	salt

1 heaping tablespoon baking powder

Use the same method as for Baking Powder Gugelhupf No. 1, beating the egg whites separately and folding them in last.

Marrow Torte

6 ozs. raw marrow (beef)	1 slice white bread
(150 g)	1/4 teaspoon nutmeg
1 3/4 cups flour	grated lemon rind and
1 egg	a few drops of lemon
1/4 cup sugar, generous	juice
1 teaspoon fat	1/4 teaspoon salt

Soak the raw marrow in cold water until all the blood comes out. Also soak the bread in water; squeeze it dry, and mash it fine with a broad knife. Next work the marrow with a wooden spoon until pliant; then work it into the flour by hand, add all the ingredients, and make a pliable dough. Roll out the dough three times, letting it rest from 1/2 hour to overnight between times. Lastly, roll out two rounds 8 - 9 inches in diameter, put poppy-seed filling between them and bake them in a 350°-400° oven for about 40 minutes.

Filling:

approximately 5½ ozs. poppy-seed

½ cup milk

sugar or honey to taste

½ cube sweet butter

¼ teaspoon or less of cinnamon

lemon rind, grated

a few chopped blanched almonds (optional)

The poppy-seed should be ground or crushed finely in a mortar and then cooked with the milk and sweetening about 10 - 15 minutes until thick. Mix in the other ingredients and cool before using.

Ready-crushed poppy-seed is now on the market, which is a great convenience; I soften it by adding ¼ cup milk, putting it over a low flame for 1 - 2 minutes, and then cooling the torte.

Carlsbad Zwieback

2½ cups flour (300 g)

½ cube butter

1 cake yeast

1 egg

1 egg yolk

½ cup milk

1 teaspoon sugar

1 teaspoon salt

Make a yeast dough, not too soft, and let it rise about 1 hour until double in bulk. Next make a roll, and put it in a long greased loaf pan, 4½ inches wide, 12½ inches long, and 2½ inches deep. Let it rise again about ½ hour or longer until light, and then bake it in a 350° oven about half an hour or until a knife comes out clean. When the loaf comes out of the oven, brush it with melted butter. The next day cut it in ½-inch slices, and toast it in the oven until brown on both sides. Keep it in a tin box, and have it handy for a cup of tea. This is especially good for a delicate stomach.

Old Bohemian Christmas Twist
(Weihnachts-Striez)

4½ cups flour, generous
    (1¼ lbs., 560 g)
⅔ cup milk
⅔ cup sugar (140 g)
2 cakes yeast
1 whole egg
2 - 3 egg yolks
1 cube butter
1 tablespoon salad oil

1 cup raisins
3 ozs. (90 g, ¾ cup)
    almonds, blanched,
    then chopped
    lemon rind
¼ teaspoon nutmeg
2 - 3 bitter ground almonds
    (optional)
1½ teaspoons salt

Make a nice dough of the above mentioned ingredients except the raisins and almonds. Beat the dough vigorously until the spoon leaves the dough and the dough looks satiny. Then mix in the raisins and almonds so that they are well distributed. Let rise until double in bulk. Put on a floured board, and divide in seven equal parts. Form a 12 - 14 inch roll of each piece and make a braid of four rolls. Then make another braid of three rolls and stick it on top and fasten with three wooden pegs. Brush with egg, let rise again until light and double in bulk, and bake in a 350° oven on a greased and dusted oven sheet for about an hour. When it comes out of the oven, brush with hot melted butter, and sprinkle generously with vanilla-flavored sugar. Do not use the same day. If the braiding causes trouble, just form a thick, long loaf and double it over.

Easter Bread (Osterlaibl)

Prepare the same way as Christmas Twist, but do not divide the dough or make a twist. Instead make a big round ball, put it in a round dish to retain the form, and make a deep incision with scissors in the middle as for hot cross buns. When it comes out of the oven, proceed as with the Twist. Do not use the same day.

Bishop's Bread

3 large egg yolks
1 cup sugar
1 cup flour
1 teaspoon baking powder
  chopped rind of 1 orange
  and a little juice

1 cup dates, figs, or raisins,
  chopped
1 cup chopped walnuts
3 egg whites, beaten stiff
  with a pinch of salt

Cream the yolks and sugar until thick. Gradually add the flour and baking powder (sifted three times) and the juice and rind. Fold in the dates and walnuts, lastly the beaten whites, and mix well. Grease a loaf pan (same as for Zwieback), and bake in a preheated oven at 325°-350° for 45 minutes or until golden brown. Turn upside down on a wire rack, and let stand overnight before cutting. If wrapped in aluminum foil, this keeps fresh for two to three weeks. This is a light fruit cake, not rich.

Skubanki

A typical Bohemian heavy dessert. Peel 1 lb. potatoes and cook them in salted water. When they are about 90 percent done, pour the water off except for 2 - 3 inches to be left in the pot. Sprinkle a cupful of flour over the potatoes and, with a wooden peg (the handle of a wooden Kochlöffel, kitchen spoon, if you have one), poke a number of holes through the flour into the potatoes. Continue cooking on a very low flame for 8 - 10 minutes. The flour should now look moist, no longer raw. If any water is left, pour it off. Mix potatoes and flour together with the back of a fork until a smooth paste develops looking like dry mashed potatoes. Now take a soup spoon dipped in hot fat and scoop out spoonful after spoonful from the mixture, dipping the spoon in hot fat every time and leveling the mixture on the spoon with your finger. Place the egg-shaped skubanki side by side on a warm platter.

When serving sprinkle ground poppy-seed and sugar over the skubanki, and liberally pour hot fat or butter over them — in Bohemia they use goose fat.

Cookies

Now that we have come to cookies, I, the translator and compiler of my mother's recipes, may be allowed to add a word in the final section of this little book. The soups, the meats, even the fine cakes, I took for granted as a child. But the cookies were special. They were child fare and much was made of them. They were also uncle fare. My mother had two old uncles, brothers of her mother, living in Paris, to whom she was greatly attached. They had come up in the world and were generous with the family. One way to show her appreciation was to make them their favorite cookies which they had known in their home village of Leschkau in Bohemia, and which were therefore called Leschkauer Eierkucherln — Leschkau Egg Cookies.

The baking of these cookies was a ceremony repeated every Christmas. Special tin boxes had to be procured for shipment. Lovingly mother placed the cookies, topped with chopped almonds and vanilla sugar, one by one onto parchment in individual layers until the box was full. My chance was to watch for those which did not have the exact nuance of brownness that made them eligible to be shipped to glamorous Paris; I was allowed to take the "burned" ones. To this day I like them a bit on the dark side.

If you want a real delicacy — try the Eierkucherln.

Fine Egg Cookies
(Leschkauer Eierkucherln)

4 cubes butter

1⅓ cups sugar (½ lb.)

4½ cups flour (560 g)

1 teaspoon baking powder

12 hard-boiled egg yolks

1 raw egg (optional)

lemon rind, grated

1 tablespoon rum

some blanched, finely chopped almonds

vanilla sugar

salt

1 raw egg yolk and 1 egg white

Cream the butter, and gradually add the sugar, the sieved or grated hard-boiled yolks, and all other ingredients except almonds, vanilla sugar, and the raw egg white. Roll out the dough, fold double. Roll out a second time, not too thin (about ½ inch thick). Cut out cookies, brush with egg white, and sprinkle each with the almonds, which have been mixed with some granulated sugar. Preheat oven to 400°, then bake on an ungreased sheet at 350° and watch carefully; they burn easily. Take them out of the oven singly as they get brown — they take about 15 - 20 minutes. After they come out, sprinkle them with vanilla sugar. If you wish, you can make the dough ahead of time; it improves when left in the refrigerator for several hours or overnight. These cookies have an excellent flavor; do not spoil them by the addition of any preserves. When first trying, use half or one-third of the recipe — the given quantities are for a large amount. If dough gets too wet, omit the raw egg.

Strawberry Cones (Skarnitzel)

1 whole egg   ¼ cup sugar (50 g)   ⅓ cup flour (40 g)

Cream the sugar with the egg until thick; mix in the flour. Put the mixture on a buttered, dusted cookie sheet in little heaps, not too close together; spread each heap evenly into thin patches, and bake quickly in a 400° oven. Remove the patches with a thin knife, and shape them into cones while they are still warm. Fill them with whipped cream mixed with chopped strawberries, and decorate with a berry.

Husarenkrapferln

1¼ cubes butter
⅓ cup sugar (70 g)
2 egg yolks
1¼ cups flour, scant (170 g)
⅛ teaspoon vanilla extract

5 - 6 blanched chopped
  almonds
1 whole egg
powdered sugar
some jam

Cream the butter, sugar, and yolks. Mix in the flour and vanilla. Form small balls, making a depression in the top of each with a thimble; brush with beaten egg, and sprinkle with the finely chopped almonds. Bake at 350° for 15 - 30 minutes until brown, and sprinkle some powdered sugar over them after baking. If you use vanilla sugar on top, you may omit the liquid vanilla. Before serving fill the depression with jam. This yields about 35 doughnut-like "Krapferl."

Macaroons (Makronen)

2 egg whites
¾ cup sugar, scant (140 g)
lemon rind, grated

5 ozs. (140 g, 1 cup) sweet
  almonds, measured,
  then ground
3 - 4 bitter almonds, ground

Beat the whites and sugar until stiff. Add the lemon rind and the blanched, dried, and ground almonds. Put the mixture on a greased oven sheet with two teaspoons, and bake in a 350° oven. If you have no bitter almonds, use some almond extract. The bitter-almond flavor is important. You can also use the kernels obtained from cracked peach or apricot pits.

Chocolate Balls No. 1

¼ lb. unsalted butter	2 tablespoons milk
2 egg yolks	½ lb. semi-sweet chocolate

Soften the butter, cream it with the yolks, add the milk and melted chocolate, and mix well. Store in the refrigerator for 1½ - 2 hours (not overnight as the mixture would get too stiff). When the consistency is right, make balls the size of a walnut, and roll them in powdered chocolate or cocoa. Place them in little paper cups such as are used for fine chocolate candy.

Chocolate Balls No. 2

⅔ cup sugar (140 g)	2 ozs. ground semi-sweet
5 ozs. (140 g, 1 cup) hazel- nuts, toasted, then ground	chocolate
	1 egg white
	1 tablespoon black coffee

Mix all the ingredients, form balls, roll in granulated sugar, and place the balls in little paper cups.

Vanilla Crescents (Vanille-Kipferln)

Prepare the vanilla sugar first. Buy a vanilla bean at the pharmacy, cut it in 3 - 4 pieces, and place in a jar with some granulated sugar. Screw the top tightly. In a few days the sugar will take on the vanilla flavor.

¼ lb. butter	2 ozs. (60 g, ½ cup)
¼ cup granulated sugar, scant	almonds, blanched, then grated
1 cup flour	vanilla sugar

Now you are ready to make the Kipferln. Mix the butter and sugar well, add the blanched, grated, dry almonds and the flour (reserving 1 - 2 tablespoons for later), and make a nice pliable dough. No salt is needed if salted butter is used. Use the remaining flour to dust your board. Form a roll 1½ inches in diameter. Cut the roll in small pieces. With the palm of your hand roll these pieces into small "sausages," 1½ inches thick, 1½ inches long. Bend them into crescents as you put them onto an ungreased cookie sheet. Bake them carefully at 350° about 10 minutes. They should remain white outside but be slightly brown on the bottom. Take them singly from the cookie sheet and roll them, while still hot, in the prepared vanilla sugar. Do not leave the kitchen for telephoning or other urgent business while the cookies are in the oven because they can burn in an instant.

Kisses No. 1

4 egg whites
1½ cups sugar (300 g)
    dry, powdered instant
    coffee to taste

2 ozs. (60 g, ½ cup) almonds,
    toasted, slivered, then
    blanched, and about
    2 - 3 ozs. (¾ cup) of
    walnut halves or chunks

Beat the whites with the sugar and instant coffee until stiff. Mix in the almonds and walnuts. Make little heaps (with two teaspoons) on a wax-paper-covered cookie sheet, and bake at 275° for about one hour; this recipe will yield 50 - 60 walnut-size balls.

Kisses No. 2

3 egg whites
½ cup sugar (100 g)

¼ cup chopped nuts
¼ cup candied fruits

Prepare the same way as Kisses No. 1.

Coconut Kisses

4 egg whites
1⅛ cups sugar, scant
    (220 g)

½ lb. shredded coconut
    (240 g)
    some lemon juice

Beat the egg whites, add the sugar, and continue beating. Then add the coconut. If too firm, add some lemon juice. Brush a cookie sheet with oil, and bake in a 250°-300° oven about 40 minutes.

Chocolate Slices

1 cube butter
2/3 cup sugar (140 g)
4 eggs, separated

3½ ozs. semi-sweet choco-
  late (100 g)
3 ozs. (90 g, ¾ cup) nuts,
  measured, then ground
⅓ cup flour (40 g)

Cream the butter, sugar, and yolks. Add the lukewarm melted chocolate and nuts. Fold in the stiffly beaten egg whites with the flour, and mix well and gently. Spread on a well-greased and dusted oven sheet (10 x 12 inches) and bake at 350° about 25 minutes. Cool. Spread a thin layer of jam on the pastry, then a chocolate icing on the jam.

Icing:

Melt about 6 ozs. semi-sweet chocolate in a double boiler. Mix with a wooden spoon until smooth. Add some oil, 1 tablespoon at a time, and continue stirring until you have the right consistency (about 4-5 tablespoons). Be sure you have no lumps. Pour over the evenly spread jam, and when cooled and completely stiff, cut into squares or strips.

The same recipe may be used for a cake. In that case, put the mixture into a cake form. After baking and cooling, cut the cake horizontally, and fill either with whipping cream or any other filling.

Round Currant Cookies (Ribiskrapferln)

1¼ cubes butter
¼ cup sugar (50 g)
2 egg yolks
2 cups flour, scant (240 g)
1 teaspoon baking powder

rind of half a lemon,
  grated
2 ozs. (50 g, ½ cup)
  almonds, blanched,
  then ground
jam

Make a pliable dough including the almonds. Cut out rounds ⅛ inch thick and about 2 inches in diameter. In half of the rounds make three holes with a thimble. Brush these with egg white, and spread a few extra ground or finely

chopped almonds over them. Bake all the rounds at 350°
until they have a nice golden color. Cool and spread currant
or any tart jam on the whole ones, and place those with
the holes on top of them. Sprinkle with vanilla sugar.

Marzipan Potatoes

16 ladyfingers (small)
   coffee or chocolate
   cream (see Pischinger
   Torte filling)
1 egg white

5 ozs., (140 g, 1 cup)
   almonds, measured,
   then ground
3/4 cup sugar, scant (140 g)
cocoa

Split the ladyfingers, and spread the flat side with
cream, and put them together again. Cut each one in 4 - 5
pieces, and then wrap the pieces in marzipan.

Marzipan:

Combine the finely ground, blanched, dried almonds with
the sugar and raw egg white. Work out very well on a sugar-
dusted wooden board until the dough no longer sticks. Roll
out thin, cut into squares the size you desire, place one piece
of the cut ladyfingers on each square, and wrap around tightly. Roll in cocoa. Make incisions in the balls to make them
look like burst baked potatoes. One can of almond paste,
or a marzipan roll, could be used instead of making the
marzipan yourself.

Jam Cookies

1 1/4 cubes butter
1/2 cup sugar (100 g)

1 2/3 cups flour (200 g)
1/8 teaspoon vanilla

Make a nice dough, and roll it out thin; cut out round
or oblong shapes and bake them quickly in a 400° oven.
When cool, spread a preserve on half the cookies, top with
the rest.

London Sticks *(Londoner Stangerl)*

1¾ cups flour (210 g)
⅓ cup sugar (70 g)
2 egg yolks
1¼ cubes butter

rind of ½ lemon, grated
salt, if butter is sweet
jam

Make a pliable dough of all the ingredients. Roll out 1 inch thick on a floured board. Place on an ungreased oven sheet or flat pan (12 x 10 inches), and bake about 30 minutes at 350° or until golden brown. Remove from the oven, spread a good tart jam evenly over the whole surface, and top with the meringue.

Meringue Topping:

4 beaten egg whites
1 cup vanilla sugar,
    scant

4 - 5 ozs. (140 g, 1½ cups)
    walnuts, measured,
    then ground

Return to the oven, and bake until the meringue is brown. Cool and cut into strips, 1 inch wide and 3 inches long, or in small squares.

Linzer Cookies

1 cube butter
1 cup flour, scant (120 g)
2 egg yolks
⅔ cup sugar, scant (120 g)
    cinnamon to taste

5 ozs. (140 g, 1 cup) un-
    blanched, toasted
    almonds, measured,
    then ground

Make a pliable dough. Roll out, and either cut with a cookie cutter or bake flat and cut into squares after removing from the oven. Bake at 350°. The cinnamon taste should be strong.

Index

131